Teacher's Resource Book

Red

Sarah Lindsay
Donna Thomson
Doug Dickinson
Series Editor: John Jackman

Nelson Thornes

Published in 2009 by:
Nelson Thornes Ltd
Delta Place
27 Bath Road
CHELTENHAM
GL53 7TH
United Kingdom

09 10 11 12 13 / 10 9 8 7 6 5 4 3 2 1

A catalogue record for this book is available from the British Library

ISBN 978 1 4085 0509 0

Illustrations by: Neil Chapman, Russ Daff, Pascale Lafond, Gustavo Mazali, Brenda McKetty, Pedro Penizzotto, Mike Phillips, Iole Rosa, Simon Rumble, Elena Selivanova, Pete Smith, Matt Ward (all Beehive Illustration) and Chris Masters

Photography by: Heather Gunn (www.heathergunnphotography.co.uk) © Nelson Thornes

Cover image: Iole Rosa (c/o Beehive Illustration)

Page make-up by Topics – The Creative Partnership, Exeter

Printed and bound in Croatia by Zrinski

Acknowledgements
The author and publisher are grateful to the following for permission to reproduce copyright material:

[Unit 1 Teach] extract from D. King-Smith, *Sophie's Adventures*, reproduced with kind permission of A P Watt Ltd on behalf of Fox Busters Ltd; [Unit 3 Talk] extract from Mary and Rich Chamberlin, *Mama Panya's Pancakes*, Barefoot Books (www.barefootbooks.com); [Unit 5 Teach] extract 'Cookie Sensations' from T. Mitton, *Senses Poems*, 1996, OUP, granted by David Higham Associates; [Unit 5 Write] *I Like* © Moira Andrew, reproduced with author's permission; [Unit 6 Teach] Extract from *Prince Cinders* by Babette Cole, Hamish Hamilton, 1987, reproduced by permissions of Penguin Books Ltd; [Unit 8 Teach] Extract from *The Sandcastle* by M.P. Robertson, published by Frances Lincoln Ltd, © 2001 reproduced by kind permission of Frances Lincoln Ltd.; [Unit 8 Write] Extract and illustrations from J. Kerr, *The Tiger Who Came To Tea*, reprinted by permission of HarperCollins Publishers Ltd. © Judith Kerr 1968; [Unit 10 Teach] *Cows*, © James Reeves from *Complete Poems for Children* (Faber Finds) reprinted by permission of the James Reeves Estate; [Unit 10 Write] *The Cow in the Storm* © Richard Edwards, reproduced with author's permission.

Every effort has been made to contact the copyright holders, and we apologise if any have been overlooked. Should copyright have been infringed in this book, the owners should contact the publishers, who will make corrections at reprint.

Contents

Reading comprehension has always been a key component in the curriculum of children of all ages, especially children of primary school age. For many years this was seen principally as a means of assessing the extent to which children were truly understanding and interpreting what they had learnt to read. However, more recently, the extent to which developing the skills of reading comprehension can help build all-important thinking skills has become apparent.

While the debate has long been joined as to whether spelling is best 'caught or taught', consideration of whether comprehension skills are 'caught or taught' has attracted little or no attention. It seems to have been accepted that if pupils are asked to answer questions on what they have read enough times, they eventually 'get it'. But do they?

Some pupils intuitively understand what they have read on several levels. The majority of pupils, however, need to be 'taught' these skills in a structured, progressive way. A pupil working individually, reading a passage and answering questions should be the final, rather than the initial, stage of the process. Helping pupils reach this final stage successfully is the basis for **Nelson Comprehension**.

To read effectively, it has been said that pupils should learn to 'read the lines, read between the lines and read beyond the lines'. In other words, they need to acquire a literal understanding of the content, without which they can hardly reach first base. All members of the class need to be helped and encouraged to achieve this goal. But beyond this, most children should be helped to develop the skills of deduction and inference, whether in understanding a story or in retrieving information in a non-fiction text, or evaluating or critically analysing what they have read.

We believe that comprehension skills are the essential building

blocks of effective learning throughout the curriculum, not just within literacy. They are crucial learning tools in most, if not all, subjects. So, should teachers take the risk that children will 'get it'?

Nelson Comprehension has therefore been given far more structure and didactic content than previous courses. Each 'unit' in the Red and Yellow Pupil Books comprises two elements: material devised to support class teaching or group work, and work offering opportunities for essential individual pupil activity. Unlike other courses, **Nelson Comprehension** unashamedly teaches comprehension. Mindful, however, of different requirements within different schools and classes, or even between different children within the same class, the content has been structured to allow flexibility so that, at the extreme, all parts of each unit can be undertaken by an individual or small group working together.

To maximise the teaching opportunities, the passages, poems and extracts have been selected to complement requirements of the range of reading required at the relevant stages of the child's development. The content is therefore not only appropriate to developing the skills of reading comprehension, but is supportive of other reading and writing requirements. Owing to the reading levels of KS1 children, extended texts from the first passage, poem or extract are often located in this Teacher's Resource Book, thus providing the flexibility to discuss the texts in greater depth. The extended texts can be accessed by the children from the whiteboard.

Nelson Comprehension, in addition, is a fully blended series. As well as the exciting and engaging (and fully self-supporting) print resources, the series is complemented with a stunning range of

ground-breaking ICT resources in which multimedia (voiceovers, sound effects, film, animations) are used to support comprehension. Not only do these further enhance the teaching and reinforcement of key comprehension skills, they also underline the fact that comprehension skills are as vital as ever in an age of electronic information, such as e-mails, internet, blogs and text messaging.

Nelson Comprehension works by using a unique two- or three-stage approach to comprehension (depending on the key stage). It starts by teaching key comprehension skills then moves into pupils' own group discussion and drama activities to reinforce their learning of the key skills. The final stage presents children with a new extract and a set of questions designed to assess what they have learnt.

Planning with Nelson Comprehension

The course covers all six primary year groups (Years 1 to 6, or Scottish P2 to P7) and each year group is split into ten teaching units. These provide coverage of the genres and text types the children will encounter in that particular year – whether fiction, non-fiction or poetry.

Each unit in **Nelson Comprehension** is linked to the exemplar planning units in the renewed National Literacy Framework. For example, Year 2 Unit 1: 'Familiar settings' is linked to Year 2 Narrative Unit 1: 'Stories with familiar settings'. Within the 'Familiar settings' unit, the familiar setting used in the two extracts is a busy town centre with a market (from *A Present for Paul*).

Each unit has a clear main objective, discussed in this Teacher's Resource Book. Full guidance is also given for the renewed Primary Literacy Framework objectives, National Curriculum assessment focuses and the Scottish Curriculum for Excellence objectives (see pages 24–27). For Red level, further links to Early Years Foundation stages are also supplied on this grid.

It is not intended that a **Nelson Comprehension** unit forms the basis for a whole framework planning unit. The work here is very much aimed at the early phases of a framework unit, in which teaching the comprehension skills relevant to a particular genre or text type is of paramount importance, prior to pupils' planning and composing their own text in the genre. The extracts are carefully chosen to engage pupils' interest and to maximise teaching and learning opportunities within a class setting. The authors consequently recommend that works from which the extracts are taken be followed up in pupils' own reading. Alternatively they could be used as whole texts for more in-depth study since they are excellent examples of the particular genre.

Carefully selected illustrated extract or storyboard to support unit focus.

Differentiated range of questions to fully support whole-class and group teaching.

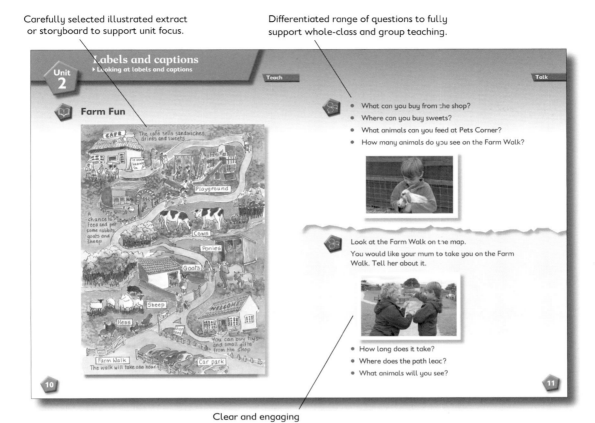

Clear and engaging illustrations.

Teach and Talk

Nelson Comprehension
Pupil Book Red
Unit 2 *Teach* and *Talk*

Each unit in the Red and Yellow Pupil Books is split into these sections: *Teach, Talk* and *Write*. The *Teach* section is designed to support whole-class or group teaching. It provides an illustrated extract to be read to the class, with introductory questions and teaching guidance supplied in this Teacher's Resource Book (see the unit by unit section, pages 28–87).

The *Talk* section then uses the same extract to support group and class work – focusing on discussion by the pupils, in order that they practise and consolidate the comprehension strategies they have just been taught. As a result, the *Talk* section in the Pupil Book provides a series of questions provided for discussion, starting with literal questions and then moving into questions that require more complex comprehension skills, such as inference and evaluation.

At Yellow level, each extract is supplied in the Teacher's Resource Book as it appears in the Pupil Book, and is fully supported with assessment and answer guidance. It also appears as an interactive multi-modal whiteboard version. However, in the Red level Pupil Book, texts are supplied in a shortened or storyboard version of the full text extract, which is provided in this Teacher's Resource Book.

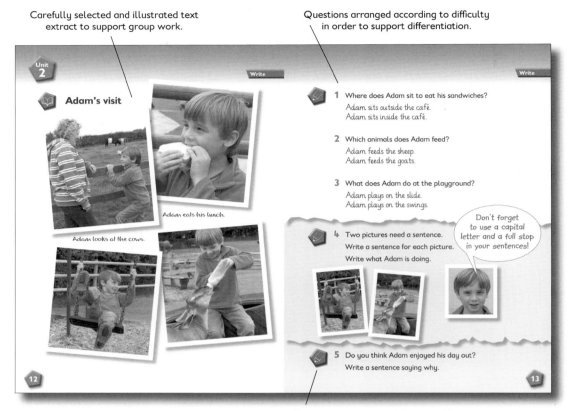

Carefully selected and illustrated text extract to support group work.

Questions arranged according to difficulty in order to support differentiation.

Group presentation activity – usually discussion, drama or composition activity.

(Red level is aimed at an age group where children will be more able to comprehend spoken text, while struggling to decode the same text on the page.) The whiteboard version of the extracts comes complete with questions, set highlights, illustrations, voiceovers, sound effects and, in some cases, animations and video.

Nelson Comprehension
Pupil Book Red
Unit 2 *Write*

Write

The *Write* section is aimed at providing individual pupils with the chance to complete a set of comprehension questions so they can be assessed on the strategies they have been taught in *Teach* and *Talk*. While the questions can obviously be used for a written test, they are equally suited for an oral question and answer or discussion activity if it is felt this is more appropriate.

Assessment and PCMs

An assessment sheet is provided in this Teacher's Resource Book for each unit's *Write* section. This includes details on the specific question type and National Curriculum assessment focuses used, so it can be used to fully support Assessment for Learning or the Assessing Pupil Progress initiative.

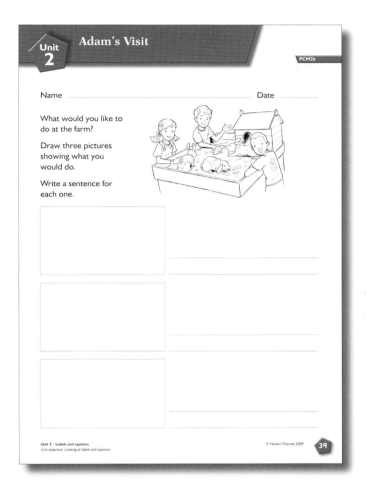

Nelson Comprehension
Teacher's Resource Book
Red
Unit 2 *PCM*

In the Red and Yellow Teacher's Resource Books, two photocopy masters are supplied with each unit as further extension work. These can be used either in class or as related homework activities.

In brief, the key pattern for KS1 **Nelson Comprehension** is:

- *Teach:* The text is introduced and presented to the children by the teacher;
- *Talk:* Pupils then discuss or answer questions on the text, either in groups or in a whole-class situation;
- *Write:* Pupils do comprehension activities individually, whether as an oral or written exercise.

Questions and differentiation

The 'prompts' or questions cover lower and higher order reading skills. Pupils are asked to respond to three basic tiers of questions:

- *A literal level*, for example, 'What was Mandy going to do if it snowed?'

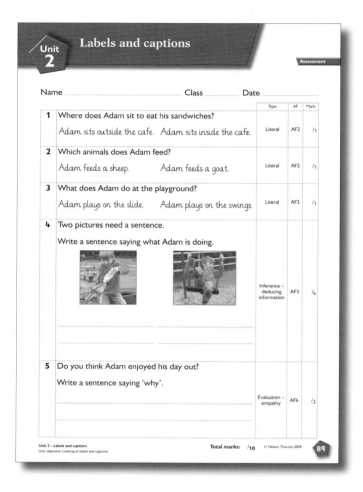

Nelson Comprehension
Teacher's Resource Book
Red
Unit 2 *Assessment Sheet*

- *An inferential level*, for example, 'How do you know that Adam was the only one excited about the snow?'

- *A personal/evaluative level*, for example, 'How do you feel about snow?'

These three core skills form the basis of further comprehension skills tested in this course. For example, literal understanding enables information finding and summarising; inference enables deduction and prediction; evaluation enables criticism, empathy and relating the child's own experience to a particular question or dilemma.

In addition, there is reference to vocabulary to encourage pupils to investigate and clarify the meanings of unknown words in context, if necessary using a dictionary. This strategy unlocks not only the meaning of the word but can have wider implications for the extract as a whole.

Introducing and rounding up

The Teacher's Resource Book unit notes on pages 28–87 include suggestions for a 'Reading' discussion in order to elicit pupils' prior knowledge, thoughts and feelings about an important aspect of the extract or text they are about to read.

After each extract there is a plenary session which is closely based on class, group or individual work and allows for the reinforcement of comprehension skills and for the unit's key objective.

Picture Snapshot Assessment

A further feature of **Nelson Comprehension** is *Picture Snapshot Assessment*, a ground-breaking method of assessing a pupil's comprehension skills using ICT-based images and animation. This technique is particularly effective with children who struggle with reading, and whose comprehension skills may be masked by the problems they have decoding text. (For full details of *Snapshots*, see pages 98–109.)

Glossary of comprehension terms

There are many comprehension terms that relate to the key comprehension strategies. Below are definitions of these terms, accompanied by an example of how they might be used as a comprehension question or statement.

Analysis
Identifying and commenting on the organisation, style or features of a text. Understanding the relationship between context, meaning and wording.

The playscript includes a <u>cast list</u>, <u>scene description</u>, <u>character parts</u> and <u>stage directions</u>.

Deduction
Judgement made from <u>inferred clues</u> to form a <u>conclusion</u>.

He realised the <u>show was over</u> when he walked in because he <u>heard applause</u> and <u>saw the actors bowing</u>.

Evaluation – *Personal meaning, empathy, response, opinion*
Looking at 'the bigger picture' – what you think from your own experience that explains the actions, feelings and motives of characters and links to information and mood within a narrative. Expressing and justifying an opinion based on information given.

I think the boy was <u>uneasy</u> about dancing <u>with Emily</u> because he <u>grimaced</u> and <u>stood</u> as <u>far away</u> from her as possible. I say that because the <u>teacher told him</u> to dance with her and Tom <u>didn't like being told</u> what to do. He was also probably <u>embarrassed</u> that the <u>other boys</u> were watching him.

Inference – *Implied and hidden meaning*
Thinking and searching for clues – providing evidence for deductions in answer to questions that ask *'How do you know that?'* or *'Why?'* Using information that is implied within the text but not given directly, from which connecting evidence is drawn to support deductions.

Q: Can the dragon breathe fire? How do you know?
A: <u>Yes, the dragon can breathe fire because smoke is coming from his nostrils</u> and <u>he has burned the trees next to his lair</u>.

Literal – *Explicit meaning*
Information is obvious and needs no interpretation (Who? What? Where? Right there!). The information is given directly on the page without need for inferring or evaluating to deduce an answer.

Q: <u>What colour</u> is the dragon?
A: The dragon is a <u>bright shade of green</u>.

Clarification – *Making sense of; making meaning clear*
Defining a word, phrase or concept as it is used in the text. Using appropriate language that accurately and meaningfully describes scenes, events, moods, actions and feelings expressed in a story or non-fiction text when retelling in own words.

Q: 'Use <u>appropriate language</u> that <u>accurately and meaningfully</u> describes scenes and events.' Explain what is meant by 'appropriate language' here.
A: I think 'appropriate language' here means <u>choosing words carefully</u> to <u>convey the same meaning</u> that was used in the text to describe the scenes and events.

Prediction
Anticipating cause and effect from implied, hidden and personal meaning within the text. Giving evidence-based reasons for what you think might have happened before, might be happening now or what might happen next to characters and events in a story.

Q: What will happen next?
A: I think the man <u>walking under the ladder</u> will get <u>covered in paint</u> because the worker <u>above him</u> has just <u>tipped over a tin of paint</u>.

Prior knowledge and experience
Personal history-based understanding, use of what you have already learnt or experienced in your own life to predict or explain the meaning of something.

Q: It was a <u>hot spring day</u> on the <u>Cornish coast</u>. Why do you think the boy <u>preferred to stay out of the sea</u> and make sandcastles even though he thought the water <u>looked inviting</u>?
A: I think the boy preferred to stay out of the sea on a hot spring day even though he thought the water looked inviting because he knew that the <u>sea was usually too cold</u> for swimming during <u>springtime in Cornwall</u>.

Summarising / retelling
Gathering, organising and presenting key points of a story or non-fiction information in the correct sequence. Using the basic story structure of beginning, middle and end, a summary or retelling involves a person, action, place, problem and resolution.

The story is about a <u>boy</u> who is <u>playing on a beach</u> in <u>Cornwall</u> on a spring day. <u>He</u> wants to <u>go swimming in the sea</u> but the <u>water is too cold</u> so <u>he makes sandcastles instead</u>.

Using Nelson Comprehension ICT
Doug Dickinson

Doug Dickinson has worked in primary education for over 40 years, and is currently a lecturer at Leicester University and a primary ICT consultant for a number of primary ICT publishers, having worked for the National Literacy Strategy and Becta.

ICT and comprehension

Since Caxton, ordinary people have been decoding and trying to make sense of the printed word; they have brought their own interpretation to authors' texts and this has led, at times, to some amusing and some disastrous incidents. Today's texts look and feel different; they are not simply composed of words on a page but often come with drawings, photographs and diagrams all interlaced together to form a comprehensive whole.

As we move further into the 21st century, the power of electronic communication in all of our lives becomes more and more evident. Today, many developed texts written to be read for information and for pleasure are multimodal, arriving with the reader in an electronic format that contains all of the printable aspects of the past but also allows for sound, video and animation on pages that can be interrogated, zoomed, hyperlinked. This is a media-rich age, and it is the understanding, the putting into perspective and the dealing with the inferences of the texts presented that is the current life skill of comprehension.

It is the comprehension (the understanding) of all of these types of text that is the function of this exciting software package, which comes complete with age-grouped examples to help readers get the best out of the fiction and non-fiction that influences and excites their learning and recreation.

Teach

The aim of the *Teach* section is to provide a teacher with fully interactive whiteboard support for the teaching of key comprehension skills.

Each *Teach* section contains an illustrated extract, which comes with click-on highlights and question boxes. Each highlight either specifically answers the particular question or, in the case of an inference question, provides clues before offering possible answers/free type for the teacher (thereby offering a three-stage process: question – clues – possible answers; this is vital for teaching children inference, deduction and 'reading between the lines').

Teachers can also make their own annotations on the extract by using their own interactive whiteboard tools or the tools provided.

The readers engage with the quality text, perhaps in a whole class or group setting, or as a guided read displayed on an interactive whiteboard. Using the annotation tools (which dock to the left of the text, but which can also be moved to any position on the screen), the text can be explained and key points emphasised.

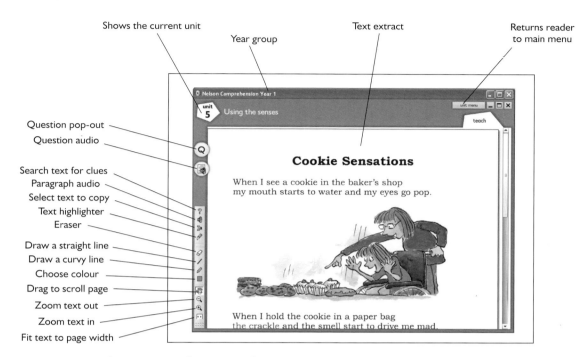

Shows the current unit
Year group
Text extract
Returns reader to main menu

Question pop-out
Question audio

Search text for clues
Paragraph audio
Select text to copy
Text highlighter
Eraser
Draw a straight line
Draw a curvy line
Choose colour
Drag to scroll page
Zoom text out
Zoom text in
Fit text to page width

Teach screen,
CD-ROM Red Unit 5

The questions for comprehension are accessed by clicking the 'Question pop-out'. Each question is intended to guide a reader towards understanding of the text by requiring one of a range of comprehension skills, such as literal understanding, inference, deduction or evaluation. Clues within the text can be accessed (and become highlighted in the text) by clicking on the 'Show clue' button.

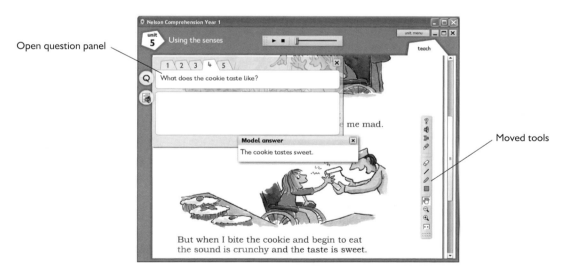

Open question panel

Moved tools

Answers to the questions can be inputted into the answer panel by clicking on the 'A' button. This opens a free writing panel. It is possible to copy and paste from the text into this panel if this is appropriate. A model answer is available for each question by clicking on the 'Model answer' button. This is intended as a guide and isn't necessarily the only answer – certainly, evaluation questions may well induce very different but equally plausible answers.

This *Teach* page has the capacity to utilise many multimedia functions to further learning and enrich comprehension (or to provide visual and audio to support a struggling reader). For example, the picture or the words can be toggled on or off (using the button in the bottom right of the picture or in the top left for the words), the sound can be switched on or off, and various other electronic supports, by way of video and animation, can all assist in the comprehension of the whole text. This multimedia provision facilitates different 'layers' of meaning – so, by adding or taking away images, voiceover or sound effects, a passage can be made easier, more difficult, or more accessible to children with different learning styles or to struggling readers with strong thinking skills.

Talk

The aim of the *Talk* section is to provide activities for children to work on in small groups – providing a stimulus for speaking and listening, drama and discussion – in order to reinforce important comprehension skills.

This section offers a new illustrated text extract and breakout activities for pairs and small groups of children to engage in supported and motivating discussion/ role play/drama scenarios, based on a static extract screen (which may have illustrations). This is clearly a 'speaking and listening' activity.

The different activities can be amended (with imported assets or typed over script) in order to make work more or less challenging, or perhaps to fit a different piece of text.

Character / object grid (including thesaurus)

The 'Character grid' gives an opportunity for a group or class to develop vocabulary to describe characters in the text and place them within zones of relevance. By doing so, it stimulates the children to explore key characters, to empathise with their situation, to evaluate their character within the story, as well as to extend their descriptive vocabulary. The grid is also used with story settings and objects of inherent importance to the texts.

The top four buttons on the default toolbar allow users to move between edit, move and interact, delete, and draw and annotate functions. Each function has its separate set of extra tools to add exciting, personalised dimensions to the activity.

The excellent 'Media bank' is accessed from the 'edit' toolbar (◠).

Another feature available from the 'Media bank' which allows for creativity in this section is the 'avatar maker'. Accessing this allows users to create and mould their own characters to be represented in the 'Character grid'.

The 'Character grid' also has a 'thesaurus' tool, which supports users in selecting appropriate words for the zones. Words from the thesaurus can be copied and pasted into a zone or it can be searched for suitable synonyms, thus extending user vocabulary.

The main text for the activity can always be accessed for reference by clicking on the text tab.

Story map

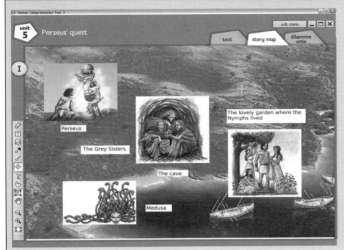

The 'Story map' uses similar functionality to the 'Character grid'. It allows users to review the text, identifying key events in sequence, and confirm their understanding by annotating the adjustable text blocks. It can also be used like a diagram with label and caption boxes.

Question maker

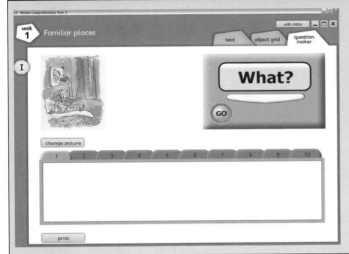

The 'Question maker' allows users to generate questions about characters and situations. The 'questioners' use the 'I' button on the screen to get instructions about the activity, together with the 'question generator' (which provides the 'Who?', 'What?', 'How?', 'Why?', 'When?' and 'Where?' question starters). They type their questions into the answer boxes (clicking on the tabs in turn) and then the character, in role, provides the answers. The skill of creating the right questions to find the information or answers they wish to know is of immense importance in developing key comprehension skills.

Each unit that utilises the 'Question maker' has its own set of instructions providing range and depth of activity.

Dilemma vote

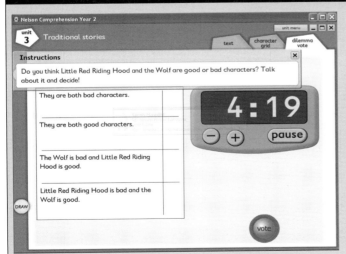

The readers are presented with a dilemma from a new text which they discuss and then vote on several options. There is a 'free type' option to give the group the opportunity to develop their own ideas. The dilemma could involve prediction, or evaluating and giving an opinion, or using inference to deduce an answer.

The default time for discussion is set to five minutes but this can be altered to suit the local situation.

In a class situation, the groups decide if they want to add another option and, once this has been agreed, start the timer and discuss the dilemma. Ideally, some of these discussions could be digitally recorded so that the quality of the discussion could be reviewed and each person's part in it evaluated. This would also support the collection of evidence of speaking and listening for APP (Assessing Pupil Progress).

When the discussion time is ended the individuals in the group then vote on their personal choice of solution to the dilemma. The idea is that they vote based on the arguments they have heard in the discussion time. To vote they simply click on the 'vote' button and the 'ballot box' will appear. They then place their 'X' next to their choice of solution and click the 'ballot box' again. An animation will show that their vote has been cast! To see how the votes add up simply click on the 'chart' button.

Info categoriser / Sequencer

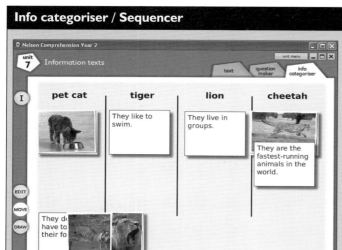

Info categoriser

This amazingly powerful application allows users to organise their knowledge gained from their understanding of the text. Each of the prepared facts or images can be edited and placed into the frameworks provided. The boxes can be edited, so the 'Info categoriser' can actually be used as a planning or research tool for further written work. As a tool it is ideal as a means to test a pupil's ability to analyse and organise information.

Clicking on the 'I' button gives instructions for the activity.

Sequencer

The 'Sequencer' allows users to do exactly what it says – sequence events or ideas in words or pictures. It can be effectively used as a full-scale writing planner. Each of the items already added to the sequence can be edited and moved by accessing the buttons on the bottom right of the screen and extra items can be added into the blanks provided. Like the 'Info categoriser', the edit feature takes the activity beyond sequencing, allowing its use as a text planning tool, or as a way to retell or summarise a text extract. Clicking on the 'I' button gives instructions for each unit activity.

Media bank

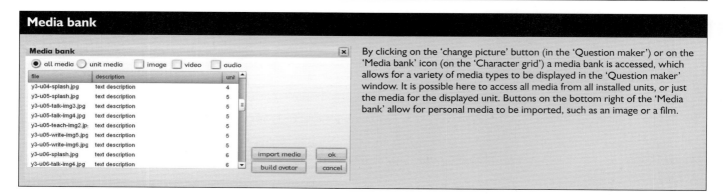

By clicking on the 'change picture' button (in the 'Question maker') or on the 'Media bank' icon (on the 'Character grid') a media bank is accessed, which allows for a variety of media types to be displayed in the 'Question maker' window. It is possible here to access all media from all installed units, or just the media for the displayed unit. Buttons on the bottom right of the 'Media bank' allow for personal media to be imported, such as an image or a film.

Text formatter

Make a playscript, Write a letter, Write insructions, Make an advert, Make an explanation, Make a poster

The 'Text formatter' allows users to create text-based contexts where the focus is on the quality of the literacy expressed through an understanding of the genre and the context of the unit. In the case of 'Make a playscript' the options allow a child to do just that, by providing playscript blocks on demand (for example, cast lists, scene descriptions and dialogue) so the child can focus on creating the content – whether it's transforming a prose passage into a playscript or creating another scene of the playscript.

The other text formatters work in a similar way and also allow the importation, through the 'Media bank', of images for illustration, which are particularly important in the case of 'Make an advert' or 'Make a poster'. The 'Text formatter' is ideal to support a child in understanding and analysing the organisation and structure of different text types.

Supporting assessment with Talk *activities*

Talk activity	Comprehension skills	Related AFs
Dilemma vote	prediction; inference; evaluation – opinion, empathy; historical/cultural context	AF2, AF3, AF6, AF7
Character/object grid	analysis – language use; evaluation – opinion, empathy; historical/ cultural context	AF5, AF7
Question maker	literal; inference; evaluation	AF2, AF3, AF6
Info categoriser	inference; analysis – text structure	AF3, AF4
Sequencer	summarising; analysis – text structure	AF2, AF4
Story	map visualisation; summarising; analysis – text structure	AF2, AF4
Text formatter	analysis – text structure/language use; inference; prediction; evaluation	AF3, AF4, AF5, AF6

Write

The aim of this section is to provide a means of reviewing the Pupil Book *Write* activities as a class/group in order to reinforce and build on the skills taught and learnt in the unit as a whole. This section is provided with a separate, but complementary, illustrated text (which can also be used as a teaching tool if teachers prefer) with around 10 questions of different types. The focus here, as in *Teach,* is on the use of the extract–questions–clues–blank–model answer sequence as a way of reviewing the children's written or even oral answers.

The tools available are complementary to those available in the *Teach* section of each unit, so as well as the 10 set questions (with highlights and clues) there is the option for the teacher or a pupil to make their own annotations and highlights on the text extract.

Picture Snapshot Assessment

The 'Picture Snapshot Assessment' is an exclusively electronic means of assessing a struggling reader's comprehension and thinking skills using visual images or animations (often accompanied by audio effects) as a basis for questions. This section is also supplied with an assessment tool that can be used as a basis for future planning for an individual pupil's needs.

The assessments here are based on users showing their ability to comprehend and answer questions that demonstrate literal, evaluation, inference, prediction and classification understanding. A simple summary is available of the results to sit alongside the evidence gathered for APP. For full details of the 'Picture Snapshot Assessment', see pages 98–109 of this book.

Nelson Comprehension and Assessment for Learning
Donna Thomson

Comprehension is a fundamental component of reading. Children need to understand that alongside 'accurate decoding of text', 'reading involves making meaning from content, structure and language' (QCA, 2006). However, children do not learn these skills without instruction. To become fluent readers they must not only be taught how to decode words accurately but also learn how to understand and interpret the author's meaning.

Assessing Pupil Progress

Comprehension assessment provides teachers with a wealth of information and is central to effective teaching and learning. The primary purpose for asking readers a range of comprehension questions is to find out what they need to be taught to support their understanding of text. Comprehension assessment offers teachers an insight into a reader's depth of thinking during and after reading. It tells them whether they are making sense of incoming information; whether they are able to infer, evaluate and justify responses to questions about the text; and how much they understand and are able to personally relate to the author's meaning.

The assessment focus (AF) criteria used to help teachers to assess pupils' reading progress clearly reflect the importance of comprehension in the development of good reading skills. Six out of the seven National Strategy assessment focuses refer to comprehension competencies and are directly linked to the criterion of National Curriculum levels (see the National Strategy grid).

Assessing Pupil Progress (APP) provides teachers with an effective structure for tracking children's learning and helps them to tailor their teaching to meet the needs of developing readers. It helps teachers to identify weaknesses and strengths through day-to-day and periodic assessment in relation to specific assessment focuses, and enables them to monitor the impact teaching and planning from AF evidence has on other areas of the pupils' learning. Intervention using these indicators raises standards of attainment in reading and across the curriculum, which in turn improves SATs results and ensures that children experience a smoother transition to secondary education.

Gathering assessment focus evidence for APP

Children's written responses to comprehension provide easy access to AF evidence. The **Nelson Comprehension** series provides a focus for this evidence using a range of quality extracts and carefully thought-out questions that support the teaching of the comprehension strategies.

However, in practice much of the evidence that is gathered in order to check a child's reading level and progression occurs in passing, through discussion and questioning about texts – particularly in Key Stage 1.

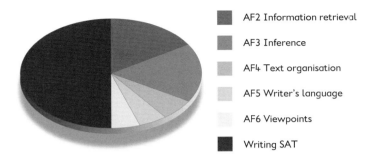

- AF2 Information retrieval
- AF3 Inference
- AF4 Text organisation
- AF5 Writer's language
- AF6 Viewpoints
- Writing SAT

2008 SATs
Marks break-down

The range of extracts and activities within the **Nelson Comprehension** series offer an excellent opportunity for discussion and oral responses to questions, particularly the *Teach* and *Talk* sections. Guided and shared reading offer valuable opportunities for teachers to explore a range of fiction and non-fiction through discussion and questions that help to develop and monitor children's understanding of text. Another activity that guides and develops comprehension is Reciprocal Reading (Palicsar and Brown, 1986), recommended by the Revised National Strategy, 2006. The 'Picture Snapshot Assessment' (see the CD-ROMs and pages 98–109 of this book) offers a means of building these skills.

Other speaking and listening activities that enable teachers to assess children's comprehension on a day-to-day basis are as follows:

- retelling from stories, a newspaper report or instructions, etc., where children are required to select the main ideas, sequence them correctly and say them coherently in their own words (AFs 2, 3, 4)

- drama, where children re-enact something they have read that relies on gathering and organising key information, interpretation and sequencing skills (AFs 2, 3, 4)

- 'hot-seating', where children act out characters from a story and others ask them questions that they need to answer in character role – in as much detail as possible – which draws on main and inferred ideas from story, interpretation of character and ideas, deduction and reference to text (AFs 2, 3, 4, 6).

There are examples of all these types of activity within the **Nelson Comprehension** series, and these are supported by the ICT Talk activities on the CD-ROM – such as the sequencer, the info categoriser, the dilemma vote and the question maker (for more details see 'Using Nelson Comprehension ICT' on pages 14–19).

Assessment focuses are also linked to different types of comprehension question and answer. For example, literal questions ask the children to locate the main 'who?', 'what?', 'where?', 'when?' information from text to answer questions (AF2). Inference questions ask children to infer, deduce and provide evidence for their answers from text (AF3). Evaluation questions ask the children to empathise with characters using their own life experience and knowledge to explain the characters' behaviour or possible motives (AF6), and clarification questions ask about vocabulary and the author's use of language (AF3 and AF5).

Each unit comes with its own assessment sheet, providing the 'Write' questions and activities along with guidance on question type, relevant assessment focus and a helpful marking system that can help inform your judgement on how well a child is using his/her comprehension skills. These can be found on pages 88–97 of this Teacher's Resource Book.

AF	AF description	Skills covered
AF2	Understand, describe, select or retrieve information, events or ideas from texts and use quotation and reference to text	literal, information finding, summarising
AF3	Deduce, infer or interpret information, events or ideas from texts	visualisation, inference, deducing information, prediction, clarification, drawing on prior knowledge
AF4	Identify and comment on the structure and organisation of texts, including grammatical and presentational features at text level	analysis of text structure
AF5	Explain and comment on writers' uses of language, including grammatical and literary features at word and sentence level	analysis of language use
AF6	Identify and comment on writers' purposes and viewpoints, and the overall effect of the text on the reader	evaluation – empathy, author viewpoint, opinion, criticism, previous experience
AF7	Relate texts to their social, cultural and historical contexts and literary traditions	evaluation – social, cultural, geographical and historical contexts

Full reading assessment guidelines are supplied on the DCSF Standards site.

Although reading and written comprehension is key to assessing children's depth of thinking, range of vocabulary and understanding of text, there are a number of children this does not suit because they struggle when decoding words on the page. They may have good inference skills, a rich verbal vocabulary and impressive understanding of the author's intention in discussion about text that has been read to them. However, these high-level skills are unlikely to be reflected in their responses to questions when they have had to read the text by themselves. As a result, they are likely to be assessed as 'poor' readers when it is actually their decoding that has failed at this level, rather than their 'whole' reading ability. It is important, therefore, that pupils can be assessed as much for their ability to infer, evaluate and comprehend the author's meaning, as they are for their decoding ability.

Nelson Comprehension's 'Snapshot Assessment' (see pages 98–109) offers an innovative solution to the problem of assessing the comprehension skills of struggling decoders. It also provides an effective comprehension measure for more able decoders who may already be assumed to be 'good readers' simply on the basis that they have fluent word recognition.

Using Nelson Comprehension with other curricula

Assessment for Learning and reading comprehension are at the heart of all the primary national curricula. As well as the English Primary National Literacy Strategy and Assessing Pupil Progress, the Scottish Curriculum for Excellence, the revised Northern Irish Curriculum for Key Stages 1 and 2, and the new

Welsh Key Stage 1 and 2 Curriculum all emphasise the need for the following key elements of assessment for learning:

- Sharing learning intentions with the children.

- Using day-to-day observation, along with discussion, oral activities and written activities, when assessing a child's comprehension skills.

- Adjusting teaching according to each child's assessment needs arising from these formative assessments.

In addition, the importance of comprehension skills to a pupil's development at primary level is inherent in the reading, talking and listening objectives of all the national curricula. This is the case even more so today than previously, as all have had, or are undergoing, substantial revisions.

Northern Ireland Key Stage 1 objectives	Foundation Phase Framework for Children's Learning* (Wales)
Talking and Listening **Nelson Comprehension** offers opportunities to engage with the following objectives: • Listening and responding to a range of fiction, poetry, drama and media texts. • Taking part in drama activities, including role play and improvisation, and making use of digital technology. • Listening to, telling, retelling and interpreting stories based on memories, personal experiences, literature and imagination. **Reading** **Nelson Comprehension** offers opportunities to engage with the following objectives: • Engaging with a range of traditional and electronic texts, which include stories, poems and informational materials, and discussing them with the teacher and others. • Reading and understanding a range of traditional and electronic texts. • Retelling, re-reading and acting out familiar poems, stories and other assorted texts. • Exploring familiar stories and other simple texts with the teacher, using drama, art and discussion to focus on features, e.g. characters, places, events and ideas. • Beginning to use evidence from text to support their views; for example, predicting, inferring and deducing. • Exploring pictures and illustrations in books, magazines and electronic sources. • Showing some understanding of the way texts are structured by representing ideas through drama, pictures, diagrams and ICT.	**Nelson Comprehension** at Red and Yellow levels supports the following foundation phase outcomes: **Foundation Phase Outcome 4** In this phase, children: • begin to extend their ideas or accounts by including some detail • respond to poems, stories and non-fiction, sometimes needing support. **Foundation Phase Outcome 5** In this phase, children: • understand and convey simple information • usually listen carefully and respond to a wider range of stimuli • show understanding and express opinions about major events or ideas in stories, poems and non-fiction • develop ideas in a sequence of connected sentences. **Foundation Phase Outcome 6** In this phase, children: • begin to modify their talk to the requirements of their audience, varying use of vocabulary and level of detail • explore and communicate ideas, showing awareness of sequence and progression in range of contexts • show they have listened carefully through relevant comments and questions • respond to texts and express preferences • show an understanding of the main points and talk about significant details • use knowledge of the alphabet to locate books and find information.

* Key Stage 1 will be replaced in 2009/2010 by extending the Foundation Phase to cover 5 to 7-year-olds. However, Nelson Comprehension at Red and Yellow levels offers opportunities to progress children's oracy and reading skills from Key Stage 1 levels 1 to 3.

For links to the Renewed Primary Literacy Framework and the Scottish Curriculum for Excellence, please see individual unit descriptions.

Unit	Unit name	Skills	Genre/text type	Extracts	Renewed framework objectives
1	Familiar settings	Exploring events and characters in a setting	Stories with familiar settings	*Sophie's Snail* Dick King-Smith *Tim's Bedtime*	**2** *Listening and responding* • Listen with sustained concentration, building new stores of words in different contexts. **7** *Understanding and interpreting texts* • Identify the main events and characters in stories, and find specific information in simple texts. **8** *Engaging with and responding to texts* • Visualise and comment on events, characters and ideas, making imaginative links to their own experiences.
2	Labels and captions	Looking at labels and captions	Labels, lists and captions	*Farm fun map* *Adam's visit*	**2** *Listening and responding* • Listen with sustained concentration, building new stores of words in different contexts. • Listen to and follow instructions accurately, asking for help and clarification if necessary. **7** *Understanding and interpreting texts* • Identify the main events and characters in stories, and find specific information in simple texts. **8** *Engaging with and responding to texts* • Distinguish fiction and non-fiction texts and the different purposes for reading them.
3	Stories from home and far away	Exploring the use of patterned and predictable language	Stories from a range of cultures; texts using patterned and predictable language	*Mama Panya's Pancakes* Mary and Rich Chamberlin *It Sounds Like An Owl* John Jackman	**2** *Listening and responding* • Listen with sustained concentration, building new stores of words in different contexts. **7** *Understanding and interpreting texts* • Identify the main events and characters in stories, and find specific information in simple texts. • Explore the effects of patterns of language and repeated words and phrases. **11** *Sentence structure and punctuation* • Use capital letters and full stops when punctuating simple sentences.
4	Instructions	Understanding instructions	Instructions	*Banana split* *Time for a drink*	**2** *Listening and responding* • Listen to and follow instructions accurately, asking for help and clarification if necessary. **7** *Understanding and interpreting texts* • Recognise the main elements that shape different texts. **8** *Engaging with and responding to texts* • Distinguish fiction and non-fiction texts and the different purposes for reading them.
5	Using the senses	Exploring senses through poetry	Poetry	*Cookie Sensations* Tony Mitton *I Like* Moira Andrew	**1** *Speaking* • Interpret a text by reading aloud with some variety in pace and emphasis. **7** *Understanding and interpreting texts* • Explore the effect of patterns of language and repeated words and phrases. **8** *Engaging with and responding to texts* • Visualise and comment on events, making imaginative links to their own experiences. **9** *Creating and shaping texts* • Find and use new and interesting words and phrases.

Early learning goals	Scottish C for E objectives	NC assessment focuses*	Comprehension skills	ICT Talk activities
Listen with enjoyment and respond to stories. Use language to imagine and recreate roles and experience. Write own names and other things, begin to form simple sentences.	**Listening and Talking** *Understanding, analysing, evaluating (first/second levels)* Responds to literal, inferential, evaluative types of questions; asks different types of questions. **Reading** *Understanding, analysing, evaluating (first/second levels)* Shares thoughts about characters and/or setting, and relates them to own experiences.	AF2, AF3	*Literal* *Visualisation*	Sequencer Dilemma vote
Show understanding of how information can be found in non-fiction texts to answer questions. Write own names and other things such as labels and captions, begin to form simple sentences. Read range of common words and simple sentences independently.	**Listening and Talking** *Understanding, analysing, evaluating (first/second levels)* Shows understanding and responds to literal, inferential, evaluative and other types of questions, and by asking different kinds of questions. **Reading** *Understanding, analysing, evaluating (first/second levels)* Shows understanding across different areas of learning; identifies and considers the purpose and main ideas of a text; uses supporting detail.	AF4, AF7, *AF2, AF3, AF6*	*Literal* *Inference* – deducing information *Evaluation* – opinion	Sequencer Story map
Interact with others, taking turns in conversation. Show understanding of elements of stories, such as character and sequence of events. Write names and other things, begin to form simple sentences.	**Listening and Talking** *Understanding, analysing, evaluating (first/second levels)* Shows understanding and responds to literal, inferential, evaluative and other types of questions. **Reading** *Understanding, analysing, evaluating (first level)* Shares thoughts about structure, characters and/or setting; Comments on the effective choice of words and other features.	AF3, AF7, *AF2, AF4*	*Literal* *Inference* *Analysis* – text structure	Character grid Sequencer
Sustain attentive listening, responding with actions. Attempt writing for different purposes, such as lists and instructions. Show understanding of how information can be found in non-fiction texts.	**Listening and Talking** *Finding and using information (first/second levels)* Select ideas and relevant information, organise these in a logical sequence and use words which will be useful for others. **Reading** *Understanding, analysing, evaluating (first/second levels)* Shows understanding across different areas of learning; identifies and considers the purpose and main ideas of a text; uses supporting detail.	AF2, AF4, *AF3*	*Literal* – summarising *Inference* *Analysis* – text structure	Info categoriser Sequencer
Listen with enjoyment and respond to poems. Enjoy listening to and using language, and turn to it in their play and learning. Use language to recreate experiences. Explore and experiment with sounds, words and texts.	**Listening and Talking** *Understanding, analysing, evaluating (first/second levels)* I can show my understanding of what I listen to or watch by responding to different kinds of questions. **Reading** *Understanding, analysing, evaluating (first level)* Shares thoughts about structure, characters and/or setting; recognises the writer's message and relates it to own experiences; comments on the effective choice of words and other features.	AF2, AF5, *AF3*	*Literal* *Visualisation* *Evaluation* – personal experience	Info categoriser Question maker

* N.B. AFs in italic are links in questions and are in addition to main AFs.

Unit	Unit name	Skills	Genre/text type	Extracts	Renewed framework objectives
6	Traditional fairy tales	Exploring characters and events in traditional stories	Traditional stories	*Prince Cinders* Babette Cole *Cinderella*	**3** *Group discussion and interaction* • Take turns to speak, listen to others' suggestions and talk about what they are going to do. **4** *Drama* • Explore familiar themes and characters through improvisation and role-play. **7** *Understanding and interpreting texts* • Identify the main events and characters in stories, and find specific information in simple texts. • Make predictions showing an understanding of ideas, events and characters. **8** *Engaging with and responding to texts* • Visualise and comment on events, characters and ideas, making imaginative links to their own experiences.
7	Recounts	Understanding recounts and ordering events	Recounts	*Our visit to the dinosaurs* *My naughty dog!*	**1** *Speaking* • Tell stories and describe incidents from their own experience in an audible voice. **7** *Understanding and interpreting texts* • Identify the main events and characters in stories, and find specific information in simple texts. • Recognise the main elements that shape different texts. **8** *Engaging with and responding to texts* • Visualise and comment on events, characters and ideas, making imaginative links to their own experiences.
8	Fantasy worlds	Exploring characters and events in fantasy stories	Fantasy stories	*The Sandcastle* M.P. Robertson *The Tiger Who Came to Tea* Judith Kerr	**3** *Group discussion and interaction* • Take turns to speak, listen to others' suggestions and talk about what they are going to do. **4** *Drama* • Explore familiar themes and characters through improvisation and role-play. **7** *Understanding and interpreting texts* • Make predictions showing an understanding of ideas, events and characters. • Use syntax and context when reading for meaning. **8** *Engaging with and responding to texts* • Visualise and comment on events, characters and ideas, making imaginative links to their own experiences.
9	Information texts	Understanding information texts	Information texts	*Being a friend* *Sorting out an argument*	**3** *Group discussion and interaction* • Ask and answer questions, make relevant contributions, offering suggestions and take turns. **7** *Understanding and interpreting texts* • Recognise the main elements that shape different texts. • Make predictions showing an understanding of ideas, events and characters. **8** *Engaging with and responding to texts* • Distinguish fiction and non-fiction texts and the different purposes for reading them.
10	Pattern and rhyme	Exploring pattern and rhyme in poetry	Poetry	*Cows* James Reeves *The Cow in the Storm* Richard Edwards	**1** *Speaking* • Interpret a text by reading aloud with some variety in pace and emphasis. **2** *Listening and responding* • Listen with sustained concentration, building new stores of words in different contexts. **7** *Understanding and interpreting texts* • Explore the effect of patterns of language and repeated words and phrases. **8** *Engaging with and responding to texts* • Visualise and comment on events, making imaginative links to their own experiences.

Early learning goals	Scottish C for E objectives	NC assessment focuses	Comprehension skills	ICT Talk activities
Retell narrative in correct sequence. Show understanding of elements of stories, such as character and sequence of events. Write various things and begin to form simple sentences, using punctuation.	**Listening and Talking** *Tools for listening and talking (first level)* Explores how pace, gesture, expression, emphasis and choice of words are used to engage others, and uses what he/she learns. **Reading** *Enjoyment and choice (first level)* Explains preference for certain texts and authors.	AF4, AF7, AF2, AF3, AF6	*Literal* *Inference* *Evaluation –* opinion	Character grid Dilemma vote
Sustain attentive listening, responding with relevant comments. Retell narrative in correct sequence. Use language to recreate experiences.	**Listening and Talking** *Finding and using information (first/second levels)* Selects ideas and relevant information, organises these in a logical sequence and uses words which will be interesting and/or useful for others. **Reading** *Tools for reading (first level)* Uses knowledge of sight vocabulary, phonics, context clues, punctuation and grammar to read with understanding and expression.	AF3, AF5, AF2	*Literal* *Visualisation*	Sequencer Story map
Show understanding of main elements of story, such as main character and sequence of events. Interact with others, taking turns in conversation. Begin to form simple sentences	**Listening and Talking** *Understanding, analysing, evaluating (first level)* Shows understanding by responding to different kinds of questions. **Reading** *Understanding, analysing, evaluating (first level)* Shows understanding and responds to different kinds of questions and other close reading tasks.	AF2, AF3	*Literal* *Visualisation*	Story map Dilemma vote
Show understanding of how information can be found in non-fiction texts to answer questions. Begin to form simple sentences.	**Listening and Talking** *Finding and using information (first level)* Identifies and discusses the purpose, key words and main ideas of the text, and uses this information for a specific purpose. **Reading** *Understanding, analysing, evaluating (first level)* Shows understanding across different areas of learning, and identifies and considers the purpose and main ideas of a text.	AF2, AF3, AF4, AF6	*Analysis –* text structure *Literal* *Inference* *Evaluation* – previous experience	Character grid Info categoriser
Listen with enjoyment and respond to poems. Enjoy listening to and using language, and turn to it in their play and learning. Explore and experiment with sounds, words and texts.	**Listening and Talking** *Tools for listening and talking (first level)* Explores how pace, gesture, expression, emphasis and choice of words are used to engage others. **Reading** *Tools for reading (first level)* Uses knowledge of sight vocabulary, phonics, context clues, punctuation and grammar to read with understanding and expression.	AF1, AF2, AF3, AF5, AF6	*Literal* *Inference* *Analysis –* language use *Evaluation –* opinion	Info categoriser Settings grid

- Who is the main character in the story?
- When does the story happen?
- Where does the story happen?
- What happens to the snail?

Sophie's snail is sucked down the plug hole.

- How do you think Sophie feels?
- Why does Sophie feel like this?

What do you think happens next?

Unit 1

Familiar settings

▶ Exploring events and characters in a setting

Sophie's Snail

Sophie had a snail race with her brothers. Sophie's small yellow snail had won the race. She loved her snail and decided to keep it as a pet...

All that evening Sophie played with her snail. When it was bedtime, and she was ready to wash and do her teeth, she put the snail carefully on the flat rim of the wash basin.

Then (as she always did) she filled the basin with warm water right up to the **overflow** and washed her face and hands. The snail did not move, though it appeared to be watching.

Then (as she always did) she brushed her teeth very hard, making a lot of **froth** in her mouth and spitting the bubbly blobs of toothpaste out on top of the rather dirty water. The toothpaste blobs made strange shapes on the surface of the water, often like a map of the world. Tonight there was a big white **Africa** at one side of the basin.

Then (as she always did) she pulled the plug out, but as she turned to dry her hands the sleeve of her dressing gown scuffed the rim of the basin. Right into the middle of the disappearing Africa fell a small yellow shape, and then the last of the whirlpooling frothing water disappeared down the plug hole, leaving the basin quite empty.

Sophie plodded down the stairs.

"My snail's gone down the plug hole," she said in a very quiet voice.

Sophie's Snail, Dick King-Smith

Extracts

Sophie's Snail Dick King-Smith

Tim's Bedtime

Planning

Stories with familiar settings

Objectives

Renewed Primary Literacy Framework Year 1

2 *Listening and responding*
- Listen with sustained concentration, building new stores of words in different contexts.

7 *Understanding and interpreting texts*
- Identify the main events and characters in stories, and find specific information in simple texts.

8 *Engaging with and responding to texts*
- Visualise and comment on events, characters and ideas, making imaginative links to their own experiences.

Assessment focuses

AF2 Understand, describe, select or retrieve information, events or ideas from texts and use quotation and reference to text

- **L1** Recalls some simple points from familiar texts;
- **L2** Recalls some specific, straightforward information, using evidence from the text.

AF3 Deduce, infer or interpret information, events or ideas from texts

- **L1** Shows reasonable inference at a basic level, e.g. identifying who is speaking in the story;
- **L2** Shows simple, plausible inference about events and information, using evidence from the text.

Scottish Curriculum for Excellence: Literacy

Listening and Talking

Understanding, analysing, evaluating (first/second levels)
Responds to literal, inferential, evaluative types of questions; asks different types of questions; comments with evidence on content and form.

Reading

Understanding, analysing, evaluating (first/second levels)
Shares thoughts about characters and/or setting, and relates them to own experiences.

TEACH

This unit helps to build children's skills in recalling events, prediction, visualisation and drawing on their own experience.

Reading

Encourage the children to look carefully at the pictures in the Pupil Book. You can use the extract from *Sophie's Snail* to support the work in this unit.

ICT

- Read the extract to the children, either in groups or as a class. The extract can be shown on the whiteboard or photocopied so the children can follow the text as it is being read and discussed.

- Discuss the words in bold. What do they mean? Which have the children heard before?

rim	The flat edge around the top of a sink.
overflow	A hole where, if too much water has been put in a sink, the water flows away. This stops the extra water spilling onto the floor.
froth	The foam that is in your mouth when you brush your teeth.
Africa	A very large area of land. It is shaped rather like an upside-down pear.

- You might like to introduce the following terms. These will be revisited later in the course.

Setting	Where does this part of the story take place? *In the bathroom.*
Character	Who is involved? Who is the main character? *Sophie.*
Event	What happens? *Sophie washes herself and cleans her teeth and then, by accident, knocks her pet snail down the plug hole.*

- Check the children's understanding of the extract by asking further questions.

What colour is Sophie's snail?

Where did Sophie put her snail while she was washing?

What did she do first – wash her face or clean her teeth?

What happened to the sink?

TALK

Discussion

Discuss the extract, either as a class or in groups. Answer the questions.

- Who is the main character in the story? *Sophie is the main character in the story.*

- When does the story happen? *The story takes place in the evening.*

- Where does the story happen? *The story is set in the bathroom of Sophie's house.*

ICT

Copy the right answers.

1 What does Tim do first? He fills the sink.
He washes his face.

2 Does Tim wash his face before he brushes his teeth?
Yes No

3 What does Tim do after he brushes his teeth? He washes his face.
He pulls out the plug.

> What do you do when you get ready for bed?

4 Write three things you do before you get into bed.

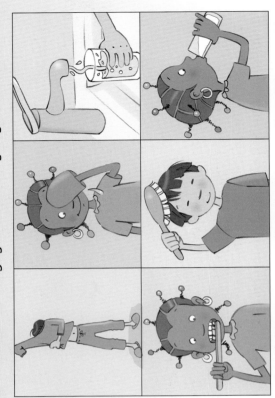

Unit 1

Tim's Bedtime

> This is what I do when I go to bed.

I fill the sink with water.

I wash my face.

I brush my teeth.

I pull out the plug and then go to bed.

They can discuss their own experiences and how these differ from other people's experiences.

Comparisons of what children do can be made by asking the children to stand in groups showing how many children brush their teeth first, how many children read a book, and so on.

ICT

Answer guidance

1 *Tim fills the sink.*
2 *Yes.*
3 *He pulls the plug.*
4 Write three things you do before you get into bed.
   This activity requires the children to think about what what they do when they get ready for bed and the order in which they do them. Encourage them to write simple sentences. Introduce the words *first, then* and *finally* explaining how they help to show the order in which things are done.

Extra

PCM1b can be used to support activity 4. Less able children could orally comment on what they do and draw picture prompts to represent their own experiences. Encourage more able children to add detail to their written sentences.

PCM

TALK *continued ...*

● What happens to the snail?
  The snail was put on the side of the sink, but Sophie accidentally knocked it into the water where it was sucked down the plug hole.

● Give the children **PCM1a**. Remind them of the extract from *Sophie's Snail* before the children match the words with the correct picture. This reinforces their understanding of the extract or, if the extract has not been used, challenges the child to use picture and word cues in order to link them correctly.

PCM

● The children are then asked to discuss how Sophie feels when her pet snail falls down the plug hole. Talk about each of Sophie's faces and what it might represent, e.g. *happy, sad, surprised, frightened.* Which best suits how Sophie felt when the snail fell down the plug hole? Discuss why Sophie feels like this, the bond she has made with the snail, etc. The children should be encouraged to empathise with the main character.

● As a group or in pairs, encourage the children to think about what Sophie might do next. Look at the possibilities suggested by the artwork but also ask the children to come up with their own ideas. Ask the children to illustrate their best idea in their own picture. Explore Sophie's character through role-play and improvisation.

Plenary

As a class or in groups review the children's answers to the questions. It is important children can identify the main character and setting. If they are struggling with this they can be encouraged to not only find evidence by listening to the story but also by looking carefully at the pictures.

What characters do they see? Where is the action happening? Discuss how they used their own experiences to answer the questions and to understand Sophie's feelings.

WRITE

Questions

● This short passage illustrates in both words and pictures what Tim does to get ready for bed each night. Where possible this extract is intended to be used for individual or small group work.

● The questions in this section establish whether the children can identify the main elements in this extract. Ask the children to answer the questions individually, then review their answers.

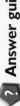

ICT

Round-up

As a class or in groups review the children's answers to the questions. They can then recount the events based on their own experience, reading aloud their three simple sentences or showing their pictures.

Sophie's Snail

Name _____   Date _____

Draw a line so the right words go with the right picture.

Sophie washes
her face.

The snail falls
into the water.

Sophie puts the snail on
the sink.

Sophie brushes
her teeth.

Unit 1 – Familiar settings
Unit objective: Exploring events and characters in a setting

Name _____ Date _____

What do you do when you get ready for bed?

Write three simple sentences and draw three pictures.

First _____

Then _____

Finally _____

- What can you buy from the shop?
- Where can you buy sweets?
- What animals can you feed at Pets Corner?
- How many animals do you see on the Farm Walk?

Look at the Farm Walk on the map.

You would like your mum to take you on the Farm Walk. Tell her about it.

- How long does it take?
- Where does the path lead?
- What animals will you see?

Unit 2

Labels and captions

▶ Looking at labels and captions

Farm fun

The café sells sandwiches, drinks and sweets

A chance to feed and pet some rabbits, goats and sheep

Playground

Cows

Ponies

Goats

Sheep

Hens

WELCOME

You can buy toys and small gifts from the shop

Car park

Farm Walk
The walk will take one hour

Extracts

Farm fun
Adam's visit

Planning

Labels, lists and captions

Objectives

Renewed Primary Literacy Framework Year 1
2 Listening and responding
• Listen with sustained concentration, building new stores of words in different contexts.
• Listen to and follow instructions accurately, asking for help and clarification if necessary.
7 Understanding and interpreting texts
• Identify the main events and characters in stories, and find specific information in simple texts.
8 Engaging with and responding to texts
• Distinguish fiction and non-fiction texts and the different purposes for reading them.

Assessment focuses
AF4 Identify and comment on the structure and organisation of texts, including grammatical and presentational features at text level
  L1 Has some awareness of meaning of simple text features, e.g. labels.
  L2 Has some awareness of use of features of organisation.
AF7 Relate texts to their social, cultural and historical contexts and literary traditions
  L1 Distinguishes a few basic features of information texts.
  L2 Identifies general features of a few text types.

Scottish Curriculum for Excellence: Literacy
Listening and Talking
Understanding, analysing, evaluating (first/second levels)
Shows understanding and responds to literal, inferential, evaluative and other types of questions.
Reading
Understanding, analysing, evaluating (first/second levels)
Shows understanding across different areas of learning; identifies and considers the purpose and main ideas of a text; uses supporting detail.

TEACH

This unit focuses on using the medium of labels, lists and captions. This consolidates children's understanding that writing carries meaning and helps them develop the concept of a sentence.

Reading

• Spend time looking at labels around the classroom. Ask the children to read them, explaining why something might have been given a label, e.g. scissors.
• Look at the *Farm Fun* map with the children. Ask them to highlight things they notice. The map can be shown on the whiteboard or photocopied so the children can refer to it as it is being discussed.
• Ask the children to read the labels on the map. Discuss the items with captions, highlighting the extra information these provide for the reader and the fact they are written in sentences.

TALK

Discussion

• Look at the map, either as a class or in groups. Answer the questions. This can help reinforce the children's understanding of the role labels and captions play.
• What can you buy from the shop?
You can buy toys and small gifts from the shop.

• Where can you buy sweets?
You can buy sweets from the café.
• What animals can you feed at Pet's Corner?
You can feed rabbits, goats and sheep.
• How many animals do you see on the Farm Walk?
There are five types of animals on the Farm Walk: hens, cows, ponies, sheep and pigs.
• The children are then required to look more specifically at the Farm Walk. They are asked to imagine that they want their mother to take them on this walk and they need to persuade her.
• Encourage the children to look at all the information the map provides to help them. This might be in the form of labels, picture clues or captions. The questions will help guide the children in exploring this information.
• How long does it take?
A caption tells us that the Farm Walk takes an hour.
• Where does the path lead?
Picture clues show us that the path goes over a bridge and through a wooded area.
• What can you do in the playground?
The pictures show us that you can play on the swings, the slide, etc.

Plenary

As a class or in groups, review the children's answers to the questions. It is important they can identify the different ways information can be transformed from the map into knowledge, e.g. labels and captions. Encourage the children, if they are struggling with reading words, to find evidence by looking carefully at the pictures.

ICT

1 Where does Adam sit to eat his sandwiches?

Adam sits outside the café.
Adam sits inside the café.

2 Which animals does Adam feed?

Adam feeds the sheep.
Adam feeds the goats.

3 What does Adam do at the playground?

Adam plays on the slide.
Adam plays on the swings.

Don't forget to use a capital letter and a full stop in your sentences!

4 Two pictures need a sentence.
Write a sentence for each picture.
Write what Adam is doing.

5 Do you think Adam enjoyed his day out?
Write a sentence saying why.

Adam's visit

Adam eats his lunch.

Adam looks at the cows.

Questions

- *Adam's Visit* is a visual recount of a boy's visit to the farm park, in the form of photographs with captions. Where possible, this work is intended for individuals or small groups.

- The questions in this section establish whether the children can identify the main elements in these pictures. Ask the children to answer the questions individually, then review their answers. Emphasis is on copying the whole sentence in answer to the question.

ICT

? Answer guidance

1 *Adam sits outside the café.*

2 *Adam feeds the goats.*

3 *Adam plays on the swings.*

4 Two pictures need a sentence. Write a sentence for each picture.

This activity requires the children to think about a caption they might add to the two pictures. Encourage them to write simple sentences, reminding them that all sentences start with a capital letter and end with a full stop.

PCM

Extra

PCM2a focuses on writing lists. The picture prompts on writing lists. The picture prompts help less able children, yet there is room to add more items for the more able children.

5 Do you think Adam enjoyed his day out? Write a sentence saying 'why'?

Pupils are now asked to look at the evidence in the photos and decide whether Adam enjoyed his day out at the farm park. They need to be specific about why they have made their decision, e.g. *Adam is seen smiling in the photos; Adam looks like he is having lots of fun*, etc.

PCM2b can be used as an extension activity. Less able students could discuss their pictures and then add individual words as labels rather than write sentences. More able students should be encouraged to add detail to their sentences, e.g. expanding 'I am feeding the sheep' to 'I enjoy feeding the hungry sheep'.

PCM

Round-up

As a class or in groups, review the children's answers to the questions. How do their lists of what Adam and his family need to take on their day out vary?

The children can then recount what they would like to do at the farm park, reading aloud their captions or showing their labelled pictures. Conclude by summarising the use of labels, lists and captions. Brainstorm other times when they might be used.

Name _____   Date _____

Adam and his family are getting ready for their trip to the farm.

Write a list of things they need to take.

Boots	

Can you think of anything else?

Name _____   Date _____

What would you like to do at the farm?

Draw three pictures showing what you would do.

Write a sentence for each one.

Stories from home and far away

▶ Recognising predictable, patterned language

Mama Panya's Pancakes

A village tale from Kenya

Mama Panya sang as she kicked sand with her bare feet, **dousing** the breakfast fire.

'Adika, hurry up,' she called cheerfully. 'Today, we go to market.'

'Surprise! I'm one step ahead of you, Mama.' Adika stood in the doorway, dressed in his finest shirt and cleanest shorts.

'I'm ready.' Now Mama Panya had to hurry.

After storing her pots, gathering her bag and slipping her feet into her sandals, Mama Panya called, 'I'm ready too, Adika. Where are you?'

'Here I am, Mama – two steps ahead of you.'

He sat under the baobab tree, Mama Panya's walking stick in hand.

'Why, yes you are.' She accepted the stick and led them down the road.

'What will you get at the market Mama?'

'Oh a little bit and a little bit more.'

'Are you making pancakes today Mama?'

'You are a smart one. I guess I can't surprise you.'

'Yay! How many pancakes will you make?'

Mama fingered two coins folded in the cloth tied around her waist. 'A little bit and a little bit more.'

Rounding the corner, they saw Mzee Odolo sitting by the river. '**Habari za asubuhi?**' Mama asked softly, so she wouldn't chase away the fish.

Adika blurted out, 'We're having pancakes tonight, please come.'

'Adika,' Mama whispered in his ear.

Mzee Odolo waved back, saying, '**Asante sana** – I'll be there.' Mama quickened her pace.

'We had to invite Mzee,' Adika said, 'he's our oldest friend.'

'Hurry up, you're a few steps behind,' Mama replied.

'Look, Mama, it's Sawandi and Naiman.' Adika's friends tapped long reeds against the **thighs** of their cattle, moving them along. 'I'll be just a few steps ahead.'

'Wait, Adika!' Mama called.

Mama hadn't gone too far before he returned. 'They'd be happy to come,' Adika panted.

Mama Panya frowned, thinking about the coins in her wrap. At the market...Adika spotted his school friend Gamila at her plantain stand. 'Mama, pancakes are her favourite.'

'Now, now – don't you...' and before she could finish he ran to greet her. Mama tried to catch up, arriving just in time to hear, 'You will come, won't you?'

'Of course,' Gamila replied.

Mama shot a stare at Adika and quickly grabbed his hand, **whisking** him away.

'Mama, we'll be able to stretch the flour.'

'Ai-Yi! How much do you think I can stretch the flour, son?' Adika waved his hand in the air. 'Oh, a little bit and a little bit more.'

From *Mama Panya's Pancakes*, Mary and Rich Chamberlin

- Where are Mama and Adika going?
- Is Adika ready when Mama wants to go?
- What is Mama cooking for tea?
- How many friends do Adika and Mama meet?

Adika keeps saying
'I'm two steps ahead'.

- What is Adika like?
- Why do you think the author keeps using this phrase?

I'm two steps ahead.

Mama is looking worried in the last picture.
Why do you think she looks worried?

asante sana (uh-sahn-tay sahn-ah) means 'thank you'

Habari za asubuhi? (ha-bar-ee zah ah-suh-boo-ee) means 'What's new this morning?'

Mama (ma-ma) is a title of honour for a woman.

Mzee (mm-zay) is a title of honour for a man.

baobab tree is a large tree that stores a lot of water.

ICT

- Discuss the words and phrases in bold. What do they mean?

dousing   pouring water over or covering something

Habari za asubuhi (see above)

asante sana (see above)

thighs   the upper part of the legs, between the knee and the hip

whisking   taking someone away quickly

TALK

Discussion

- Read through the extract with the class or in groups.

- Highlight the repeated phrases in the extract (Adika: 'I'm one / two / a few steps ahead' and Mama Panya: 'A little bit and a little bit more'). Discuss the effect they have on the text – they increase the pace and highlight the characteristics of the two main characters. Answer the questions.

TEACH

This unit looks at the role of patterned language in stories. It focuses on how patterned language makes the writing more memorable, gives characters catch phrases and provides the story with pace.

Reading

- You can use the picture story in the Pupil Book either to help support the extract from *Mama Panya's Pancakes*, or on its own.

- Read the extract from *Mama Panya's Pancakes* to the children, either in groups or as a class. The extract can be shown on the whiteboard or photocopied so the children can follow the text as it is being read and discussed.

- You might like to remind the children of the following terms:

Setting   Where does this part of the story take place?

Character   Who is involved? Who is/are the main character/s?

Event   What happens?

- Give the children some background to the extract: the story is based in Kenya, and Adika and Mama Panya live in a typical Kenyan village. The language spoken in the extract is Kiswahili.

Extracts

Mama Panya's Pancakes Mary and Rich Chamberlin
It Sounds Like An Owl John Jackman

Planning

Stories from a range of cultures; using texts with patterned and predictable language

Objectives

Renewed Primary Literacy Framework Year 1

2 Listening and responding
- Listen with sustained concentration, building new stores of words in different contexts.

7 Understanding and interpreting texts
- Identify the main events and characters in stories, and find specific information in simple texts.
- Explore the effects of patterns of language and repeated words and phrases.

Assessment focuses

AF3 Deduce, infer or interpret information, events or ideas from texts

L1 Shows reasonable inference at a basic level, e.g. identifying who is speaking in the story.
L2 Shows simple, plausible inference about events and information, using evidence from the text.

AF7 Relate texts to their social, cultural and historical contexts and literary traditions

L1 Distinguishes a few basic features of stories.
L2 Shows some awareness that books are set in different times and places.

Scottish Curriculum for Excellence: Literacy

Listening
Understanding, analysing, evaluating (first/second levels)
Shows understanding and responds to literal, inferential, evaluative and other types of questions.

Reading
Understanding, analysing, evaluating (first level)
Shares thoughts about structure, characters; comments on the effective choice of words and other features.

It Sounds Like An Owl

Howl ... Howl ...
"What's that sound?
What's that loud
sound?" said Ben.

"It sounds like an owl.
It must be an owl,"
said Pen.

"Go to sleep, Ben!"

"It's not an owl. Owls don't howl!" said Ben.

Howl ... Howl ...
"What's that sound? What's that loud sound?"
said Ben.

"It sounds like a cow. It must be a cow,"
said Sue. "Go to sleep, Ben!"

"It's not a cow. Cows don't howl!" said Ben.

Howl ... Howl ...
"It's Spot! It's Spot!
Shut up Spot and go
back to the house!"

Howl! Howl!

Copy and finish the sentences.

howl

1 Ben is worried by the _____ .

    owl   howl

2 Ben thinks the howl is an _____ .

    cow   owl

3 Sue tells Ben to go to _____ .

    lie down   sleep

4 It is _____ howling.

    Spot   Ben

5 This story has a pattern.

- Copy a line that is repeated in the story.
- How many lines are repeated?

Answer guidance

1 Ben is worried by the howl.
2 Pen thinks the howl is an owl.
3 Sue tells Ben to go to sleep.
4 It is Spot howling.
5 This story has a pattern. Copy a line that is repeated in the story. How many lines are repeated?

This activity requires children to identify the pattern in the story. Ask them to re-read the story – less able children may need support with this. Children need to look carefully at the text, focusing on the pattern and repeated lines. There are three repeated lines (*Howl ... howl*; *'What's that sound? What's that loud sound?' said Ben*; *'Go to sleep, Ben!'*).

Extra

PCM3b asks children to add to the extract while continuing the patterned language. The second, more challenging half is for more able children and they may need to refer to the extract in the Pupil Book.

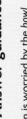

PCM

groups can be encouraged to role-play the story, repeating the key elements of the patterned language used.

Encourage children to read aloud their own versions of the patterned language from **PCM3b**.

---

sentences. More able and less able children can be paired up for this activity. Some may be able to reflect the pattern of the language highlighted to them previously.

Plenary

As a class or in groups review the children's answers to the questions. Encourage them to explain why they came up with the answers they did – what evidence did they find in the extract or pictures?

On the whiteboard, brainstorm the character traits of Adika and Mama Panya.

Ask some children to read out their continuation of the stories from **PCM3a**.

WRITE

Questions

- This extract illustrates clearly the use of patterned language in a story. Where possible this extract is intended to be used for individual or small group work.

- The questions in this section establish whether children can identify the main elements in this extract. Ask them to copy the sentences carefully, adding the missing word, then review their answers.

Round-up

As a class or in groups review the children's answers to the questions. Pupils in small

ICT

TALK continued ...

- Where are Mama and Adika going?
Mama and Adika are going to the market to buy flour.

- Is Adika ready when Mama wants to go?
Yes, Adika is ready and waiting for Mama with her walking stick.

- What is Mama cooking for tea?
Mama is cooking pancakes for tea.

- How many friends does Adika meet?
Adika meets four friends and invites them all to tea!

- Check the children's understanding of the extract by asking further questions: *How does Mama Panya put out the fire? What is Mzee Odolo doing by the river? What does Adika ask his friend Gamila? Why is Mama Panya standing by the flour in the market?*

- The children are then required to discuss Adika's character and why the author keeps repeating the phrase 'I'm two steps ahead'. *Adika is a friendly, happy, thoughtful child, warmly inviting all his friends for pancakes. The phrase is used to convey Adika racing ahead of his mum.*

- Encourage the children to feel empathy with Adika. Would they want to do the same thing?

- Now look in a little more detail at Mama Panya's character. Discuss why she is looking worried. Encourage the children to look at the pictures for clues. Adika's and Mama Panya's characters could be explored further through role-play and improvisation.

PCM

- **PCM3a** asks the children to continue the story, writing their own simple

Name _____   Date _____

Adika's friends arrive at Mama Panya's house.

What happens next?

Write a sentence next to each picture.

_____

_____

_____

_____

Here are some words to help.

Adika

Mama

pancakes

friends

fire

food

It sounds like an owl

Name ______________________ Date __________

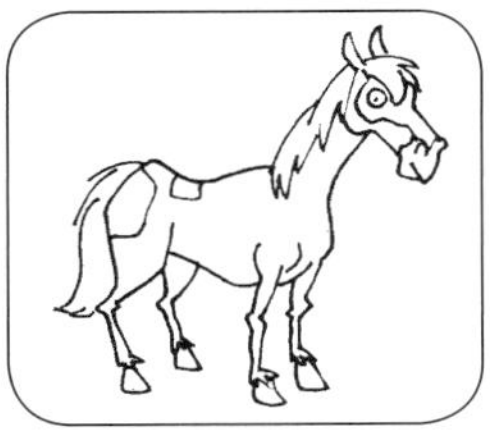

horse

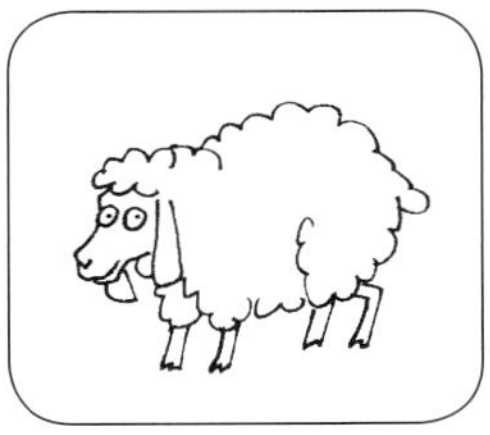

sheep

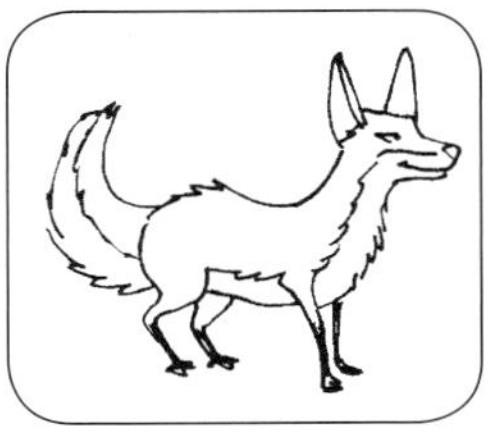

fox

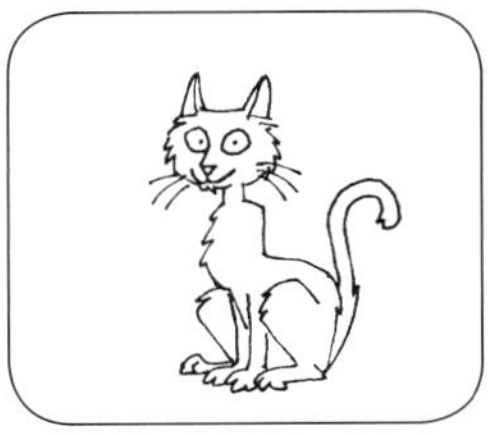

cat

Fill the gaps in the story.
Choose your own animals and names.

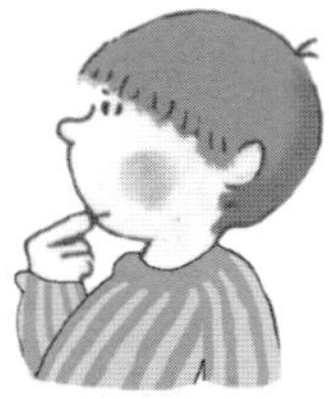

Howl … Howl …

"What's that sound? What's that loud sound?" said Ben.

"It sounds like an ____________ .

It must be an ____________ ," said ____________ .

"Go to sleep, Ben!"

"It's not an ____________ .

____________ don't howl!" said Ben.

Howl … ____________ …

"What's that sound? What's that loud sound?" said Ben.

"It sounds like a ____________ .

It must be a ____________ ," said ____________ .

"____ !"

"It's not a ____________ .

____________ don't howl!" ____________ .

Unit objective: Recognising predictable, patterned language

If you make a banana split…

- What do you do first?
- Where do you put the banana?
- What is poured over the banana and ice cream?
- When do you use the strawberries?

Look at the pictures.

- Put the instructions in the right order.

  Put the strawberries and chocolate chips on the top.

  Put the banana on a plate and put the ice cream on top of it.

  Pour the chocolate sauce over the banana and ice cream.

  Peel the banana and cut it down the middle, from the top to the bottom.

Instructions
▶ Understanding instructions

Banana split

You will need: 1 banana
2 scoops of ice cream
chocolate sauce
a few strawberries
some chocolate chips

What to do:

1 Peel the banana and cut it down the middle, from the top to the bottom.

2 Put the banana on a plate and put the ice cream on top of it.

3 Pour the chocolate sauce over the banana and ice cream.

4 Put the strawberries and chocolate chips on the top.

Your banana split is now ready to eat!

Extracts

Banana split
Time for a Drink

Planning

Instructions

Objectives

Renewed Primary Literacy Framework Year 1

2 Listening and responding
• Listen to and follow instructions accurately, asking for help and clarification if necessary.

7 Understanding and interpreting texts
• Recognise the main elements that shape different texts.

8 Engaging with and responding to texts
• Distinguish fiction and non-fiction texts and the different purposes for reading them.

Assessment focuses

AF2 Understand, describe, select or retrieve information, events or ideas from texts and use quotation and reference to text
L1 Recalls some simple points from texts;
L2 Recalls some specific, straightforward information; has a generally clear idea of where to look for information.

AF4 Identify and comment on the structure and organisation of texts, including grammatical and presentational features at text level
L1/L2 Has some awareness of meaning of simple text features.

Scottish Curriculum for Excellence: Literacy

Listening and Talking
Finding and using information (first/second levels)
Select ideas and relevant information, organise these in a logical sequence and use words which will be useful for others.

Reading
Understanding, analysing, evaluating (first/second levels)
Identifies and considers the purpose and main ideas of a text; uses supporting detail.

TEACH

This unit focuses on understanding the role of instructions and how the writing of instructions differs from descriptive sentences.

Reading

• Give the children a set of simple instructions to follow. It might be as simple as moving them from the carpet to their desks, asking them to pick up a pencil on the way. Call out the instructions in three or four stages rather than as a general request, so the children can understand what a series of instructions is like.

• Ask the children to repeat the instructions you have just given them. Highlight the fact that instructions are given or written in an impersonal way.

TALK

Discussion

• First look at the *Banana split* pictures in the Pupil Book, either as a class or in groups. Encourage the children to discuss and answer the questions.

Answering the questions ensures they fully understand the process of making a Banana split.

• If you made a Banana split, what do you do first?
First, I would peel the banana and cut it down the middle.

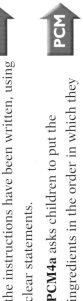

• Where do you put the banana?
The banana is put on a plate.

• What is poured over the banana and ice-cream?
Chocolate sauce is poured over the banana and ice-cream.

• When do you use the strawberries?
You use the strawberries at the end when they are put on top of the banana.

• The children are then required to order the instructions and match them with the pictures. If it is felt children may need help with this, they could be shown the version on page 40 of this Teacher's Resource Book (either photocopied or on the whiteboard), before asking them to complete the task. Highlight the fact that the children need to look for picture clues to help guide them to the appropriate instructions. Discuss how the instructions have been written, using clear statements.

• **PCM4a** asks children to put the ingredients in the order in which they are used. Less able children could be shown the recipe from page 46; more able children could be challenged to do this from memory.

Plenary

As a class or in groups, work through children's answers to the questions. It is important they can identify the way instructions are written differently from descriptive sentences.

Copy and complete the sentences.

1 The boy is making a _____.

drink   banana split

2 The boy pours squash into a _____

mug   glass

3 The boy adds water from the _____.

tap   jug

4 The boy _____ the glass of squash.

drinks   gives away

5 Write a list of what is needed to make a glass of squash.

6 Write instructions for each picture.
Here are some words to help.

first   pour

then   drink

jug

water

glass   squash

Time for a drink

Unit
4

WRITE

Questions

- The illustrations in *Time for a drink* show a child making a drink of squash.

- Encourage children to look carefully at the pictures in order to extract all the relevant information needed.

- Where possible, this work is intended for  individuals or small groups.

- The tasks in this section establish whether the children can identify the main elements in these pictures. The children are required to copy the sentence and add the missing word to complete it. Ask them to answer the questions individually.

Answer guidance

1 The boy is making a *drink*.
2 The boy pours squash into a *glass*.
3 The boy adds water from the *jug*.
4 The boy *drinks* the glass of squash.
5 Write a list of what is needed to make a glass of squash.

The children are asked to list what is needed in order to make the squash. To do this, encourage them to look carefully at the pictures, e.g. glass, water, squash. Less able children could draw the individual items instead of listing them.

Extra

PCM4b is provided to structure the writing of the answers needed in questions 5 and 6. The word prompts will help less able children. It brings together all the elements of information needed in order to provide appropriate instructions for making a glass of squash.

6 Write instructions for each picture. Here are some words to help.

This activity requires children to write instructions to complement the pictures. Again, remind them of the different writing style for instructions. Some words have been provided to give support in the spelling of words, as well as helping support the children's ideas.

Round-up

As a class or in groups review the children's answers to the questions. Compare the different ways the instructions to the drink activity have been written.

For fun, divide the children into pairs and ask them to write short instructions for other activities of their choice, e.g. brushing their teeth, playing tag. Ask them to try out the instructions to see if they work well.

Conclude the unit by summarising the use of instructions. Brainstorm other times when instructions might be used.

Banana split

Name _____ Date _____

Put these things in the order in which they are used when you make a banana split.

chocolate sauce   banana   strawberries   ice-cream   chocolate chips

1 _____

2 _____

3 _____

4 _____ and _____

Name _____   Date _____

Helpful words

squash	glass	water
pour	jug	drink

Making a glass of squash

What you need

_____   _____

_____   _____

How to make it

1

2

3

4

Unit 5

Using the senses
▶ Exploring senses through poetry

Cookie Sensations

When I see a cookie in the baker's shop
my mouth starts to water and my eyes go pop.

When I hold the cookie in a paper bag
the crackle and the smell start to drive me mad.

But when I bite the cookie and begin to eat
the sound is crunchy and the taste is sweet.

Tony Mitton

- What is this poem about?
- How do we know the girl wants to eat the cookie?
- Does the cookie smell nice?
- What does the cookie taste like?

Some of the words in the poem rhyme.
- Which word in the poem rhymes with **shop**?
- Which word in the poem rhymes with **eat**?

Read the poem.
Think of actions for the poem.
Read the poem out loud and add your actions.

My mouth starts to water and my eyes go pop.

Extracts

'Cookie Sensations' Tony Mitton

'I Like' Moira Andrew

Planning

Poetry: using the senses

Objectives

Renewed Primary Literacy Framework Year 1

1 Speaking
- Interpret a text by reading aloud with some variety in pace and emphasis.

7 Understanding and interpreting texts
- Explore the effect of patterns of language and repeated words and phrases.

8 Engaging with and responding to texts
- Visualise and comment on events, making imaginative links to their own experiences.

9 Creating and shaping texts
- Find and use new and interesting words and phrases.

Assessment focuses

AF2 Understand, describe, select or retrieve information, events or ideas from texts and use quotation and reference to text
- L1 Recalls some simple points from texts.
- L2 Recalls some specific, straightforward information.

AF5 Explain and comment on the writer's use of language, including grammatical and literary features
- L1 Comments on obvious features of language.
- L2 Notes some effective language choices; identifies some familiar patterns of language.

Scottish Curriculum for Excellence: Literacy

Listening and Talking
Understanding, analysing, evaluating (first/second levels)
Can show understanding of what is listened to or watched by responding to different kinds of questions.

Reading
Understanding, analysing, evaluating (first level)
Shares thoughts about structure, characters and/or setting; recognises the writer's message and relates to own experiences.

TEACH

This unit helps children to read and respond to poems that capture sensory experiences. They then explore their own senses, finding words to describe their own experiences.

Reading

- Read the poem 'Cookie Sensations' with the children, either in groups or as a class. The poem can be shown on the whiteboard while it is being discussed.
- Revise the five senses.
- Discuss the senses that are evident in this poem. You might like to provide the children with a cookie to munch on while discussing the words used to describe the cookie in the poem. What words would the children use to describe the biscuits they are eating?

TALK

Discussion

- Encourage the children to read the poem with you, following the rhythm and keeping time.
- Discuss the poem and answer the questions.
- What is this poem about?
  This poem is about a cookie that is seen in a shop window.
- How do we know the girl wants to eat the cookie?
  The girl says that her mouth starts to water when she sees the cookie.

- Does the cookie smell nice?
  Yes, the cookie smells so nice that the girl says it drives her mad wanting to eat it.
- What does the cookie taste like?
  The cookie tastes sweet.
- The children are then required to look carefully at the words in the poem and identify the words that rhyme:
  'pop' rhymes with 'shop'; 'sweet' rhymes with 'eat'.
- As a group or in pairs, encourage the children to think about which actions can be used to illustrate the poem. Look at the possibilities suggested by the artwork but also ask the children to come up with their own ideas.

Plenary

As a class or in groups, review the children's answers to the questions.

Encourage the groups or pairs of children to perform the poem to the class, showing the actions they have chosen.

ICT

Copy the right answers.

1 What taste does the boy like?
The taste of toothpaste.   The taste of sausages.

2 What sound does the girl like?
The sound of bells.   The sound of the fairground.

3 What sight does the boy like?
The sunshine flickering.   The fairground lights flashing.

4 This poem has a line about each of the senses.

> Can you write a poem about the things you <u>don't</u> like?

Write a poem about things you <u>don't</u> like.

Choose some things you don't like to taste, smell, feel, hear and see.

Start each line with
'I don't like the ...'

> I don't like the feel of jam slipping through my fingers.

Unit
5

I Like

I like the taste of toothpaste tingling on my tongue.

I like the smell of sausages nuzzling at my nose.

I like the feel of sunshine flickering on my face.

I like the sound of bells echoing in my ears.

I like the sight of fairground lights flashing in the dark.

Moira Andrew

WRITE

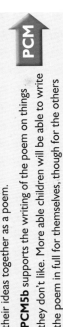

Questions

- This poem clearly defines the senses to the reader. Where possible, this poem is intended to be used for individual or small group work.

- The questions establish whether the children can identify the main elements in this poem. Ask the children to answer the questions individually, then review their answers. Encourage them to write in whole sentences.

Round-up

As a class or group, review the children's answers. The children can discuss their own experiences and how these differ from other people's.

Encourage the children to read their poems aloud.

? Answer guidance

1 *The taste of toothpaste.*
2 *The sound of bells.*
3 *The fairground lights flashing.*
4 Write a poem about things you don't like.

This activity requires the children to think about their own experiences, describing things they don't like. Introduce and discuss similes for 'like' and 'don't like', the latter often evoking more powerful feelings. The PCMs will help to structure the writing of their poem.

Extra

PCM5a can be used to organise the children's ideas into the different sense categories. Ask them to write down their ideas. It will then be easier for them to put their ideas together as a poem.

PCM5b supports the writing of the poem on things they don't like. More able children will be able to write the poem in full for themselves, though for the others this provides support in completing their own poem. Less able children can complete the poem with one word answers.

I Like

Name _____ Date _____

	Things I don't like
Taste	
Smell	
Feel	
Sound	
Sight	

Unit 5 – Using the senses
Unit objective: Exploring senses through poetry

Name _____   Date _____

Write a poem about things you don't like.

I don't like the taste of _____

_____

I don't like the smell of _____

_____

I don't like the feel of _____

_____

I don't like the sound of _____

_____

I don't like the sight of _____

_____

Unit 6

Traditional fairy tales

▶ **Exploring characters and events in traditional stories**

Teach

Prince Cinders

Prince Cinders was not much of a prince. He was small, spotty, scruffy and skinny.

He had three big hairy brothers who were always teasing him about his looks.

They spent their time going to the Palace Ball where they met other princes and princesses.

They made poor Prince Cinders stay behind and clean up after them.

When his work was done he would sit by the fire and wish he was big and hairy like his brothers.

One Saturday night, when he was washing the socks, a dirty fairy fell down the chimney …

From Prince Cinders, Babette Cole

Talk

- Is Prince Cinders good-looking?
- How many brothers does Prince Cinders have?
- Where did Prince Cinders' brothers go?
- What fell down the chimney?

- What is Prince Cinders like?
- What does he look like?
- Is he happy?
- What would he like to do?

- Which fairy tale is this story like?
- Why do you think this?

Prince Cinders Babette Cole
Cinderella

Planning

Traditional stories and fairy tales

Objectives

Renewed Primary Literacy Framework Year 1
3 Group discussion and interaction
• Take turns to speak, listen to others' suggestions and talk about what they are going to do.
4 Drama
• Explore familiar themes and characters through improvisation and role-play.
7 Understanding and interpreting texts
• Identify the main events and characters in stories, and find specific information in simple texts.
8 Engaging with and responding to texts
• Visualise and comment on events, characters and ideas, making imaginative links to their own experiences.
Assessment focuses
AF4 Identify and comment on the structure and organisation of texts, including grammatical and presentational features at text level
L1 Shows some awareness of simple text features.
L2 Shows some awareness of use of features of organisation, e.g. beginning and ending of story.
AF7 Relate texts to their social, cultural and historical contexts and literary traditions
L1 Distinguishes a few basic features of stories.
L2 Shows some awareness that books are set in different times and places.
Scottish Curriculum for Excellence: Literacy
Listening and talking
Tools for listening and talking (first level)
Explores how pace, gesture, expression, emphasis and choice of words are used to engage others.
Reading
Enjoyment and choice (first level)
Explains preference for certain texts and authors.

TEACH

This unit encourages children to explore their understanding of traditional stories, looking at characters, plot and events.

Reading

• With the children look carefully at the picture story in the Pupil Book.

• You could then read the extended extract from Prince Cinders to the children, either in groups or as a class.

• The extract can be shown on the whiteboard or photocopied so the children can follow the text as it is being read and discussed.

• Discuss the following terms in the context of the extract.

> **Setting** Where does this part of the story take place?
> **Character** Who is involved? Who is/are the main character/s?
> **Event** What happens?

TALK

Discussion

• Read through the extract with the class or in groups.

• Introduce the voice of the story as the 'narrator'.

ICT

• Discuss the setting, character and events in relationship to this extract.

• Answer the questions.

• Is Prince Cinders good-looking?
No, Prince Cinders isn't good looking.

• How many brothers does Prince Cinders have?
Prince Cinders has three brothers.

• Where did Prince Cinders' brothers go?
Prince Cinders' brothers enjoyed going to the Palace Ball.

• What fell down the chimney?
A soot-covered fairy fell down the chimney!

• This section asks the children to look more closely at Prince Cinders' character and his role in the extract. What does Prince Cinders look like? Is he happy? Discuss why. What would he like to do? Encourage the children to listen to the extract again and look carefully at the artwork for clues. Encourage the children to feel empathetic with Prince Cinders. Would they feel the same in the same situation?

PCM

• PCM6a can be used to support this activity. It requires the children to brainstorm words that describe Prince Cinders. Ask the less able children to focus on the pictures in the Pupil Book to give them ideas for words. Hot-seating can be used as an aid.

• Can the children make the link between this story and the more traditional story of Cinderella?

Copy the right answers.

1 Where did Cinderella want to go?

She wanted to go to the ball.
She wanted to go outside.

2 Who helped Cinderella?

Her sisters helped.
Her godmother helped.

3 Who did Cinderella dance with?

She danced with a friend.
She danced with the prince.

4 Did Cinderella leave the ball on time?

No, she didn't leave on time.
Yes, she left on time.

5 Which story did you like most?

Prince Cinders   Cinderella

Remember to use a capital letter and a full stop.

● Write a sentence saying why.

Cinderella

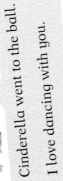

Cinderella   I want to go to the ball.

Godmother   I will help you.
You must get home at
12 o'clock!

Narrator   Cinderella went to the ball.

Prince   I love dancing with you.

Narrator   Cinderella ran from the ball.

Cinderella   I'm late!

Narrator   The shoe fitted.

Prince   I'm so happy.

Narrator   They lived happily ever after.

? Answer guidance

1 *She wanted to go to the ball.*
2 *Her godmother helped.*
3 *She danced with the prince.*
4 *No, she didn't leave on time.*

• Check children's understanding of the extract by asking further questions: *What time did Cinderella have to get home? What did Cinderella lose when she ran from the ball? How did the prince know he had danced with Cinderella? Which character says 'I will help you'? Who states 'They lived happily ever after'?*

• Highlight the difference between a playscript and a normal story. Discuss the importance of the narrator's role.

5 *Which story did you like most?*

This activity requires the children to look at the two versions of *Cinderella* and state which one they prefer. They are asked to write a sentence supporting their answer. Discuss their answers in a group, and encourage the children to take turns to speak and listen to others' conclusions.

Extra

• **PCM6b** requires the children to be aware of the traditional Cinderella story. It asks the children to look at the main characters (Cinderella and her sisters) in more detail and follow how they might be feeling at different stages in the story.

PCM

WRITE

Questions

• This extract is a simplified version of the more traditional version of *Cinderella* in the form of a play. Where possible, this extract is intended to be used for individual or small group work.

• The questions establish whether the children can identify the main elements in this extract. Ask the children to answer the questions individually, copying the correct sentence. Review their answers.

Round-up

As a class or in groups, review the children's answers to the questions.

Discuss as a larger group which story was preferred. Discover whether more of the class liked *Prince Cinders* or *Cinderella* by physically standing them in groups.

In small groups, the children can be encouraged to re-enact the *Cinderella* play or, for the more able children, a new, completed version of *Prince Cinders*.

TALK continued …

• Ask the children if they think this extract is a whole story or just the beginning. Why do they think this? They may highlight the fact that they recognise the story content. Less able children may need to be asked if this story reminds them of *Snow White* or *Cinderella*, in order to focus their thought processes.

• Ask the children to explain what clues they can find (both in the pictures and the extract) to support why they can link the extract with *Cinderella*.

Plenary

As a class or in groups, review the children's answers to the questions. Encourage them to explain why they came up with the answers they did – what evidence did they find in the extract or pictures?

Discuss the different descriptive words they found to describe Prince Cinders in **PCM6a**.

Did they enjoy this new version of *Cinderella*? How do they think the story might continue or end? Complete the story as a class or in groups with you or another adult as the scribe. Obtain a copy of the book *Prince Cinders* to read the actual ending of the story to the children.

Name _____   Date _____

Write words that tell us about Prince Cinders.

messy		

Unit 6 – Traditional fairy tales
Unit objective: Exploring characters and events in traditional stories

© Nelson Thornes 2009

Name _____   Date _____

How does Cinderella feel?
How do the ugly sisters feel?

Fill in the table.

	Cinderella	**Ugly sisters**
At the beginning of the story		
In the middle of the story		
At the end of the story		

Our visit to the dinosaurs

We had to get to school early. First, a bus took us into the town and dropped us at the museum. I cried because I felt sick.

We had to stay very close to Miss Morris so we didn't get lost.

Then we visited the dinosaurs. They weren't real, just models, but they looked real! Some of the dinosaurs moved which made some of the children scream. That made Sam and me laugh.

Later, we saw some real dinosaur bones. They were from a Triceratops. A Triceratops has three horns and can grow as long as a bus. I wish I could see a real one.

I really liked our trip to the museum. I want to go again.

by Jake

Talk

- Where are the children going?
- Why do you think Jake was crying?
- What made some of the children scream?
- How many horns does a Triceratops have?

Our visit to the dinosaurs

Talk

Some visits we go on are with our school.
Some are with our family or friends.

- Where have you been on a visit?

Tell someone else about it. Try to use these words:

first   then   after   later

Extracts

Our visit to the dinosaurs
My naughty dog!

Planning

Recounts

Objectives

Renewed Primary Literacy Framework Year 1

1 *Speaking*
- Tell stories and describe incidents from their own experience in an audible voice.

7 *Understanding and interpreting texts*
- Identify the main events and characters in stories, and find specific information in simple texts.
- Recognise the main elements that shape different texts.

8 *Engaging with and responding to texts*
- Visualise and comment on events, characters and ideas, making imaginative links to their own experiences.

Assessment focuses

AF3 Deduce, infer or interpret information, events or ideas from texts
  L1 Applies reasonable inference at a basic level.
  L2 Applies simple, plausible inference about events and information, using evidence from text.

AF5 Explain and comment on writers' use of language, including grammatical and literary features
  L1 Comments on obvious features of language.
  L2 Identifies some familiar patterns, e.g. first, next, last.

Scottish Curriculum for Excellence: Literacy

Listening and Talking

Finding and using information (first/second levels)
  Selects ideas and relevant information, organises in a logical sequence and uses interesting or useful words.

Reading

Tools for reading (first level)
  Uses knowledge of sight vocabulary, phonics, context clues and grammar to read with understanding.

TEACH

This unit focuses on recounts and ordering events, highlighting that writing is in the past tense and often uses time connectives.

Reading

- Introduce recounts. Give the children a brief recount of something that happened recently in class. Ask them, if they were to write up the incident, whether it would be a piece of fiction or non-fiction.

- Ask the children to recount something orally. Act as scribe. Discuss the importance of ordering a recount and the time connectives that might be used, e.g. *First, Next, After*, etc.

- Recounts are written in the past tense. Discuss this with the children.

- Look at the comic strip in the Pupil Book. Then, as a class or in groups, read the recount either showing it on the whiteboard or giving out photocopies to the children. Ask the children to answer the questions to help reinforce their understanding of the order in which the events of a recount may be written.

- Why do you think Jake was crying?
  Jake was crying because he felt sick.

- What made some of the children scream?
  The moving dinosaurs made some of the children scream.

- How many horns does a Triceratops have?
  A Triceratops has three horns.

- The children are then required to think of a visit they have made with family, friends or school. They are asked to tell someone else about it while using the connectives *first, then, after* and *later*. Again, this will encourage them to think about the order of a recount.

- If there is time, pupils could draw pictures illustrating different key events from their visit. The more able children could add notes including the above connectives.

Plenary

As a class or in groups, review the children's answers to the questions.

Encourage them to share their recounts, describing the incidents from their own experience in an audible voice. If any pupils speak of a shared experience, compare their recounts to show how different people have different perspectives on the same activities.

TALK

Discussion

- Where are the children going?
  The children are going to the museum.

ICT

Copy and finish the sentences.

1 Barney likes to eat _____.

books   shoes

2 _____ forgot to put his shoes away.

Dad   Barney

3 Barney chewed the shoes behind the _____.

cupboard   sofa

4 Barney wasn't told off because he looked _____.

happy   very sorry

5 Think of something that happened between you and an animal.

Write about what happened.
Remember to write it in the order things happened!

Unit 7

My naughty dog!

20th August

My dog Barney is very naughty. He eats shoes!
We need to put our shoes away as soon as we take them off so he doesn't eat them.

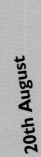

Yesterday, when Dad came home from work, he forgot to put his shoes away.
Later, I found Barney chewing Dad's shoes behind the sofa!
He looked at me with his big eyes and looked very sorry so I didn't tell him off.

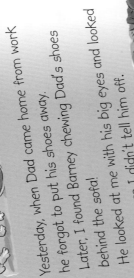

Then I put Dad's shoes away for him. I hope he doesn't see the hole Barney made in them!

WRITE

Questions

- This extract focuses on the activities of a cheeky dog. Where possible, this work is intended for individuals or small groups.

- The questions in this section establish whether children can identify the main elements in this extract. Ask them to answer the questions individually, then review their answers. They are required to copy the sentence, adding the missing word.

? Answer guidance

1 Barney likes to eat **shoes.**

2 **Dad** forgot to put his shoes away

3 Barney chewed the shoes behind the **sofa.**

4 Barney wasn't told off because he looked **very sorry.**

Extra

- **PCM7a** extends the recount of Barney and the chewed shoes. Children are asked to look at four further pictures which detail what happened next. However, the pictures are not in order and the child is required to number them correctly. More able children could add captions to the pictures, continuing the recount.

PCM

5 Think of something that happened between you and an animal.

Now the children are asked to think of something that happened between them and an animal. They are instructed to write a recount, in the order in which it happened.

PCM7b can be used to support this question 5. It provides space for the children to draw and write what happened. Less able children will add simple sentences but more able pupils should be encouraged to use more complex sentences. Remind all children to write each sentence correctly, using a capital letter and ending with a full stop.

PCM

ICT

ICT

Round-up

As a class or in groups, review the children's answers to the questions.

The children can then read out their recounts. Discuss who had the most amusing / saddest / most interesting recount.

Conclude the unit by summarising the purpose of recounts, the fact that they are written in the past tense and include connectives.

67

My naughty dog!

Name _____ Date _____

These pictures continue the story of Barney and Dad's shoes.

Number them to show the order in which they should appear.

Unit 7 – Recounts
Unit objectives: Understanding recounts and ordering events

© Nelson Thornes 2009

Name _____   Date _____

Writing a recount

Draw pictures showing what happened between you and an animal.

Write a sentence for each picture.

First _____

_____

_____

Then _____

_____

_____

Next _____

_____

_____

Finally _____

_____

Fantasy worlds

▶ Exploring characters and events in fantasy stories

The Sandcastle

There was nothing in the whole world that Jack liked better than building sandcastles. But as strong as he built the walls and as high as he built the towers, he couldn't stop the sea from stealing them away.

At the end of a perfect day, Jack looked proudly at his latest sandcastle. As the tide rolled in, he stood stubbornly in its path. 'Stay back, sea!' he ordered. 'This is my castle; I'm king here.' But the sea just spat at his knees.

Then something caught Jack's eye – a shell that **glistened** like a jewel. He placed it on the highest **turret** of his sandcastle, then shut his eyes tight.

'I wish my sandcastle was as big as a real castle and I wish that I was king,' he said.

But when he opened his eyes, his castle hadn't grown an inch and he was still just a boy on the beach.

That evening Jack was woken by the squabbling of the gulls. He drew back the curtains and rubbed his eyes in disbelief. His first wish had come true.

Jack sneaked down to the beach, and as he drew near to the castle the drawbridge lowered. Jack wasn't scared. This was his castle, so he marched across.

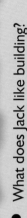

He was met at the gatehouse by a girl whose eyes were as blue as the ocean.

'We've been waiting for you,' she said. Then, placing a shell to her lips, she blew a salty note.

At her signal the doors to a great hall swung open. Jack was greeted by a **fanfare** of trumpets and was led through the cheering crowd to a seashell throne. The girl placed a pearly crown on his head.

'Hail, King Jack!' cheered the crowd. 'The king of the sandcastle.'

His second wish had come true.

The band struck up a tune and the girl led Jack into a merry **jig**. Through the night they danced. In the frenzy, no one heard the waves slapping against the great doors.

At last, the doors could no longer hold back the sea. With a thunderous crash they gave way. The ocean roared in, sweeping people off their dancing feet. As the water washed over the crowd they began to change! Jack watched in amazement as their feet became tails and their skin became scales …

From *The Sandcastle*, M.P. Robertson

- ● What does Jack like building?
- ● What does Jack want to be?
- ● Who did Jack meet outside the castle?
- ● What came in through the castle doors?

Some strange things happen in this story.
- ● Which things wouldn't happen to you in real life?

- ● What do you think happens next to Jack?
- ● How you think the story finishes?

The Sandcastle M.P. Robertson
The tiger who came to tea Judith Kerr

Planning

Stories about fantasy worlds

Objectives

Renewed Primary Literacy Framework Year 1
3 *Group discussion and interaction*
• Take turns to speak, listen to others' suggestions and talk about what they are going to do.
4 *Drama*
• Explore familiar themes and characters through role-play.
7 *Understanding and interpreting texts*
• Make predictions showing an understanding of ideas, events and characters.
8 *Engaging with and responding to texts*
• Visualise and comment on events, characters and ideas, making imaginative links to their own experiences.
Assessment focuses
AF2 Understand, describe, select or retrieve information, events or ideas from texts
L1 Recalls some simple points from texts; locates some pages/sections of interest;
L2 Recalls some specific, straightforward information.
AF3 Deduce, infer or interpret information, events or ideas from texts
L1 Makes reasonable inferences at a basic level; comments/questions on meaning of parts of text;
L2 Makes, simple, plausible inference about events and information, using evidence from text.
Scottish Curriculum for Excellence: Literacy
Listening and Talking
Understanding, analysing, evaluating (first level)
Shows understanding and responds to literal, inferential and evaluative questions
Reading
Understanding, analysing, evaluating (first level)
Shows understanding and responds to different kinds of questions and other close reading tasks.

TEACH

This unit encourages children to explore their understanding of stories about fantasy worlds, looking at characters, plot and events and comparing them with reality and their own experiences.

• Encourage the children to think about how they might react if they were Jack in the situation described in the story.

TALK

Reading

• Read the extract from *The Sandcastle* to the children, either in groups or as a class.

• The extract can be shown on the whiteboard or photocopied so the children can follow the text as it is being read and discussed.

• You can use the picture story in the Pupil Book to help support the extract. Note this is a shortened version of the extract above.

• Revisit the following terms.

Setting Where does this part of the story take place?
Character Who is involved? Who is/are the main character/s?
Event What happens?

• Discuss the words in bold. What do they mean? Which words have the children heard before?

glistened shone, like it was polished
turret a tower
fanfare a short introduction of playing trumpets
jig a lively, jumping dance

Discussion

• Discuss the setting of the story and Jack, the main character.

• Discuss how the events in the story are different from what happens in the world around us.

• Answer the questions.

• What does Jack like building?
Jack likes building sandcastles.

• What does Jack want to be?
Jack wants to be king of the castle.

• Who did Jack meet outside the castle?
Jack met a girl outside the castle.

• What came in through the castle doors?
The sea (water) came in through the castle doors.

• Check the children's understanding of the extract by asking further questions. What did Jack put on the castle he built on the beach? Do you think the shell had anything to do with Jack's wishes? What happened to the people when the water came in?

ICT

ICT

Unit 8

The Tiger Who Came to Tea.

Once there was a little girl called Sophie, and she was having tea with her mummy, in the kitchen. Suddenly there was a ring at the door. Sophie's mummy said, "I wonder who that can be …We'd better open the door and see."

Sophie opened the door, and there was a big, furry, stripy tiger. The tiger said, "Excuse me, but I'm very hungry. Do you think I could have tea with you?" Sophie's mummy said, "Of course, come in."

So the tiger came into the kitchen and sat down at the table.

Sophie's mummy said, "Would you like a sandwich?" But the tiger didn't take just one sandwich. He took all the sandwiches on the plate and swallowed them in one big mouthful. Owp!

And he still looked hungry, so Sophie passed him the buns.

The Tiger Who Came to Tea, Judith Kerr

Copy the right answers.

1 Who was Sophie having tea with?
Sophie was having tea on her own.
Sophie was having tea with her mummy.

2 What noise did Sophie hear at the door?
Sophie heard a ring.
Sophie heard a knock.

3 Who opened the door?
Sophie opened the door.
Mummy opened the door.

4 What did the tiger want?
The tiger wanted to meet Sophie.
The tiger wanted to have tea.

These words tell us about Sophie or the tiger.
Copy and sort the words to match the right character.

big   hungry   small   furry

polite   pretty

                                              stripy

Sophie

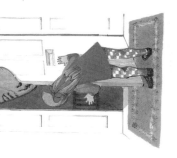

Tiger

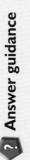

TALK continued ...

- The children are then required to identify the strange things that happen during the story. Encourage the children to listen to the extract again and look carefully at the artwork for clues. Which things wouldn't actually happen to the children in real life? For example, the sandcastle becomes a huge castle that you can walk into, Jack becomes king and the people change when touched by the water.

PCM8a supports the children with this activity. It asks the children to circle the things that would not ever happen to them. The statements are supported by artwork to aid less able children.

Finally, the children are asked to think about what might happen next and how the story might finish. Emphasise that because it is a fantasy story anything can happen! Encourage the children to use the characters already introduced in the story and describe what happens to them, rather than introducing too many more characters.

Plenary

As a class or in groups, review the children's answers to the questions. Encourage them to explain why they came up with the answers they did – what evidence did they find in the extract or pictures?

Ask the children to tell the others about their planned ending of the story. Role-play some of the children's story endings.

Obtain a copy of the book *The Sandcastle* to read the actual ending of the story to the children.

WRITE

Questions

- This extract is another example of a fantasy world. Where possible, this extract is intended to be used for individual or small group work.

- The questions in this section establish whether the children can identify the main elements in this extract. Ask the children to answer the questions individually, copying the correct sentence, then review their answers.

Round-up

As a class or in groups, review the children's answers to the questions.

Encourage the children to discuss whether they enjoy fantasy stories and why.

Share the children's stories of the tiger knocking on their door! (**PCM8b**)

Create an imaginary setting and characters with the class and, in groups, encourage the children to explore story ideas, possibly through role-play.

Answer guidance

1 *Sophie was having tea with her mummy.*
2 *Sophie heard a ring.*
3 *Sophie opened the door.*
4 *The tiger wanted to have tea.*

- Check the children's understanding of the extract by asking further questions: *What did the tiger eat first? How many sandwiches did the tiger eat? What did the tiger eat next?*

5 Copy and sort the words to match the right character. This activity requires the children to look more closely at the characters and to sort the words so that they match either Sophie or the tiger. Discuss their answers in a group. Encourage the children to take turns to speak and listen to others' conclusions. Do any of the children think that some words might fit both characters?

Extra

PCM8b asks each child to imagine they are the one who opened the door to the tiger. What would happen in the story if they were the main character? Brainstorm ideas and ask the children to draw pictures for the key events and write about them.

73

Name _____   Date _____

These things happened in the story.
Circle the things that would **never** happen to you.

Jack built a sandcastle.

Jack shouts at the sea.

Jack finds a pretty shell.

Jack makes a wish.

Jack woke in the night.

Jack goes into the big sandcastle.

Jack was made king.

Jack ran away as the water burst in.

Unit 8 – Fantasy worlds
Unit objective: Exploring characters and events in fantasy stories

© Nelson Thornes 2009

Name _____   date _____

If a tiger knocked at your door what would you do?
Draw pictures and then write what would happen.

Information texts
▶ Understanding information texts

Being a friend

Playing on your own

It is great to do things on your own.

You can play when you want to.

No one tells you what to do.

Finding a friend

Sometimes it is more fun to play with other people.

Look out for other people who like to play the same games as you.

If you pass someone and they smile at you, be brave and ask if you can play with them.

If someone looks lonely, go and ask if they would like to play a game.

Playing with friends

You can do many things with friends, like:

chat

play chase

make things

dance

play football

race.

Remember, when you play with friends – have fun!

Friends are important.

- What is this telling us about?
- Is it good to do some things on your own?
- Why do people like playing with friends?
- What things can you do with a friend?

Look at the sections.
In which section does it tell us:
- what you can do with a friend
- why it can be good to play by yourself?
- it is fun to play with other people?

The author wants to write more in her book about 'friends'.

- What else could she say?

PCM

ICT

Extracts

Being a friend
Sorting out an argument

Planning

Information texts

Objectives

Renewed Primary Literacy Framework Year 1

3 Group discussion and interaction
• Ask and answer questions, make relevant contributions, offering suggestions and take turns.

7 Understanding and interpreting texts
• Recognise the main elements that shape different texts.
• Make predictions showing an understanding of ideas, events and characters.

8 Engaging with and responding to texts
• Distinguish fiction and non-fiction texts and the different purposes for reading them.

Assessment focuses

AF2 Understand, describe, select or retrieve information, events or ideas from texts and use quotation and reference to text
  L1 Recalls some simple points about texts; locates some sections;
  L2 Recalls some specific, straightforward information; has an idea of where to look for information.
AF3 Deduce, infer or interpret information, events or ideas from texts
  L1 Makes reasonable inferences at a basic level;
  L2 Makes simple, plausible inference about events and information, using evidence from the text.

Scottish Curriculum for Excellence: Literacy

Listening and Talking
Finding and using information (first level)
  Identify and discuss the purpose, key words and main ideas of the text, and use this information for a specific purpose.

Reading
Understanding, analysing, evaluating (first level)
  Identifies and considers the purpose and main ideas of a text.

TEACH

This unit focuses on understanding non-fiction texts and how different texts can provide information. The differences in how they are organised is highlighted.

Reading

• Look at the extract *Being a friend* in the Pupil Book. The extended version can be shown on the whiteboard or photocopied so the children can follow as it is being read and discussed.

• Discuss with the children how the text is organised: information is given under sub-headings to make reference to the information easier.

• Read through the extract with the class or in groups.

TALK

Discussion

• Encourage the children to discuss and answer the questions.

• What is this telling us about?
  The information is telling us about how to be a friend.

• Is it good to do some things on your own?
  Yes, sometimes it is good to do things on your own, you can play what you want to.

• Why do people like playing with friends?
  People like playing with friends because sometimes it is more fun.

• What can you do with a friend?
  You can chat, make things, play chase, dance etc. with a friend.

• The children are then asked to look more closely at the information supplied in each section. Highlight how the children need to look for picture or written clues (if access to the full extract in this Teacher's Resource Book is available) to help guide them to the appropriate sections.

• In which section does it tell us:
  – what you can do with a friend?
    Playing with friends
  – why it can be good to play by yourself?
    Playing on your own
  – it is fun to play with other people?
    Finding a friend.

Finally the children are asked to think about what else they might include in a book about 'Friends'. What other aspects of friendship are important to them? Once topics have been thought about, ask more able children to provide possible headings for them, e.g. *Games to play with friends*, *How to play with friends*, *How to sort out an argument.*

• **PCM9a** can be used to support and extend this activity, encouraging children to draw and write about their friends, before giving details about why they think they make a good friend. These could be put together to make a class book on friendship.

Unit 9

Sorting out an argument

Here are some steps to help you sort out an argument.

1 Stop arguing.

2 Calm down. Take deep breaths.

3 Agree to talk about it.

4 Everyone gets a turn to tell, not yell, their story.

5 Think up lots of ideas to sort out the problem.

6 Choose the best idea, the one everyone agrees with.

7 Do it!

Remember, arguments are allowed, but meanness is not!

Copy and finish the sentences.

1 This _____ tells us what to do if we have an argument.

   story   information

2 The first thing you should do is _____ arguing.

   stop   keep

3 _____ must have a turn to tell their story.

   Everyone   One child

4 Choose the best _____ to solve the argument.

   story   idea

5 Have you argued with a friend?

  ● What was it about?

  ● Write some sentences saying how you felt and how you sorted it out.

Don't forget to use capital letters and full stops.

Plenary

As a class or in groups, work through the children's answers to the questions. It is important that the children can identify the different ways information texts are laid out.

Discuss in more detail how to find a friend. Ask children to order their ideas with the most important points first.

Share the children's ideas of what else might be added to the book on friendship.

Chat about why the children make good friends, referring to **PCM9a**.

WRITE

Questions

- Encourage the children to look carefully at the pictures and text in *Sorting out an argument* in order to extract all the relevant information needed. Where possible, this work is intended for individuals or small groups.  **ICT**

- The questions in this section establish whether the children can identify the main elements in the text. First the children are required to copy each sentence and add the missing word to complete it. Ask the children to answer the questions individually.

Round-up

As a class or in groups, review the children's answers to the questions.

Encourage the children to share their ideas on how best to solve arguments.

This unit could be a useful vehicle for children to express their anxieties about arguments over which they have little control, e.g. between other children when they have divided loyalties or between adults at home.

Conclude the unit by summarising the use of information texts. Brainstorm other times when they might be used.

? Answer guidance

1 This **information** tells us what to do if we have an argument.
2 The first thing you should do is **stop** arguing.
3 **Everyone** must have a turn to tell their story.
4 Choose the best **idea** to solve the argument.
5 The children are then required to consider the questions: *Have you argued with a friend? What was it about?*

Encourage children to think about an argument they have had with a friend and write a few sentences explaining how the argument was sorted out. A more able child could provide detail, possibly ordering and numbering what happened. A prompt is provided, reminding children to use capital letters and full stops.

Extra

PCM9b is an extra activity designed for more able children, looking at the vocabulary that has been used in this unit. The children are asked to match the words with their correct meanings. They may need support to read the definitions.

 ICT

PCM

Name _____   Date _____

Draw two of your friends.

Write some things that you like about them.

_____

_____

_____

_____

What makes you a good friend?

_____

_____

Unit 9 – Information texts
Unit objective: Understanding information texts

Name _____   Date _____

Match the words with their meanings.

friend   doing something to make
                                    someone feel better

help   time spent doing fun things

lonely   someone you like

play   someone who is afraid to meet
                                    or speak to anyone

shy   someone who does not have
                                    anyone to talk to

'Time to go,' said the brown cow.
'Ah,' said the white.
'Nice chat.' 'Very pleasant.'
'Night.' 'Night.'

Half the time they munched the grass, and all the time
    they lay
Down in the water-meadows, the lazy month of May,
A-chewing,
A-mooing,
To pass the hours away.

James Reeves

- What is the weather like?
- What do the cows have to eat?
- Which cow sees the rain coming?
- Do you think the flies worry the cows?

Listen to the poem again.
- Do you like this poem? Why?
- Do you have a favourite line?

Unit 10

Pattern and rhyme
▶ Exploring pattern and rhyme in poetry

Cows

Half the time they munched the grass, and all the time
    they lay
Down in the water-meadows, the lazy month of May,
A-chewing,
A-mooing,
To pass the hours away.

'Nice weather,' said the brown cow.
'Ah,' said the white.
'Grass is very tasty.'
'Grass is all right.'

Half the time they munched the grass, and all the time
    they lay
Down in the water-meadows, the lazy month of May,
A-chewing,
A-mooing,
To pass the hours away.

'Rain coming,' said the brown cow.
'Ah,' said the white.
'Flies is very tiresome.'
'Flies bite.'

Half the time they munched the grass, and all the time
    they lay
Down in the water-meadows, the lazy month of May,
A-chewing,
A-mooing,
To pass the hours away.

Poems

'Cows' James Reeves
'The Cow in the Storm' Richard Edwards

Planning

Poetry – pattern and rhyme

Objectives

Renewed Primary Literacy Framework Year 1

1 Speaking
- Interpret a text by reading aloud with some variety in pace and emphasis.

2 Listening and responding
- Listen with sustained concentration, building new stores of words in different contexts.

7 Understanding and interpreting texts
- Explore the effect of patterns of language and repeated words and phrases.

8 Engaging with and responding to texts
- Visualise and comment on events, making imaginative links to their own experiences.

Assessment focuses

AF1 Use a range of strategies, including accurate decoding of text, to read for meaning
- **L1** Reads some high frequency and familiar words fluently and automatically; awareness of punctuation.
- **L2** Shows some fluency and expression when reading.

AF2 Understand, describe, select or retrieve information, events or ideas from texts and use quotation and reference to text
- **L1** Recalls some simple points from texts.
- **L2** Recalls some specific, straightforward information; has a generally clear idea of where to look for it.

Scottish Curriculum for Excellence: Literacy

Listening and Talking
Tools for listening and talking (first level)
Explore how pace, gesture, expression, emphasis and choice of words are used to engage others.

Reading
Tools for reading (first level)
Uses knowledge of vocabulary, phonics, grammar, etc, to read with understanding and expression.

TEACH

This unit helps children to read and respond to poems that rhyme and have simple patterned stories. They will explore how sounds, words and phrases are used and sequenced while looking at poems with a similar theme.

Reading

- Read the poem 'Cows' (found above) to the children, either in groups or as a class.

- The poem can be shown on the whiteboard or photocopied so the children can follow the poem as it is being read and discussed.

- Discuss the picture shown in the Pupil Book, highlighting what the children might smell, see, touch, etc. if they were there.

- Read the poem in time as if a cow were slowly chewing its cud. Discuss the pace of the poem with the children.

- What do the cows have to eat?
  The cows have grass to eat. The brown cow thinks the grass is 'very tasty'. The white cow thinks it is 'all right'.

- Which cow sees the rain coming?
  The brown cow sees the rain coming. ('Rain coming,' says the brown cow.)

- Do you think the flies worry the cows?
  The cows don't like the flies, because they bother them and bite them.

- Encourage the children to listen again to the poem. Discuss what they like or dislike about the poem. Why? Are there any lines that particularly stand out to them?

PCM

- **PCM10a** can be used as an aid in recording the children's thoughts. Less able children may need support in recording their responses.

Plenary

As a class or in groups, review the children's answers to the questions.

Discuss the pace of the poem and the link with the actions of a cow chewing.

Highlight the verse that is repeated four times. Encourage the children to join in with this verse – the less able group might like to say the 'A-chewing, A-mooing' lines.

TALK

ICT

Discussion

- Discuss the poem either as a class, in small groups or pairs. Answer the questions.

- What is the weather like?
  The weather in the poem is pleasant, but there are rain clouds in the distance.

Unit 10

The Cow in the Storm

The sky turned grey,
The horse went 'Neigh',
But the cow just went on chewing.

The sky turned black,
The ducks went 'Quack',
But the cow just went on chewing.

Lightning sparked,
The farm dogs barked,
But the cow just went on chewing.

Raindrops splashed,
The farm cats dashed,
But the cow just went on chewing.

Showers stopped,
Rabbits hopped,
But the cow just went on chewing.

Sunshine streamed,
The whole farm steamed,
But the cow,
The cow,
The cow,
The cow, just went on chewing.

Richard Edwards

Copy the right answers.

1 What is the cow doing?

The cow is sleeping.
The cow is chewing.

2 What sound does the duck make?

Quack
Neigh

3 What do the dogs do?

The dogs dash.
The dogs bark.

4 When does the sun come out?

At the start of the poem.
At the end of the poem.

5 Rhyming words

Which word rhymes with:

black?	grey	quack	chewing
barked?	sparked	steamed	dashed
stopped?	neigh	splashed	hopped

6 Which cow poem do you like the best?

Reading

- Highlight the 'cow' link between the two poems.

- Encourage the more able children to read 'The Cow in the Storm' themselves. Read the poem aloud to or with less able children.

ICT

Questions

The questions in this section establish whether the children can identify the main elements in this poem. Ask the children to answer the questions individually, then review their answers.

Round-up

As a class or in groups, review the children's answers to the questions.

The children can comment on which of the two poems is their particular favourite, explaining why. They can discuss what they like or don't like about the poems.

Do they know any other 'cow' poems?

ICT

? Answer guidance

1 *The cow is chewing.*
2 *Quack.*
3 *The dogs bark.*
4 *At the end of the poem.*

- The children are then required to look carefully at the poem, identifying rhyming words from three alternatives: *'black' rhymes with 'quack';* *'barked' rhymes with 'sparked';* *'stopped' rhymes with 'hopped'.*

- Which cow poem do you like the best?

More able children will be able to write simple sentences in response to this question, and less able children should be encouraged to give an oral account. Again **PCM10a** can be used as an aid in recording the children's thoughts on the poems.

PCM10b can be used to ensure the children have understood the sequence of the poem 'The Cow in the Storm'. This could be used in place of PCM10a for less able children.

PCM

Name _____ Date _____

Do you like this poem?   Yes   No

Why?

Finish the sentences.

I like _____

_____

I don't like _____

_____

My favourite line in the poem is _____

_____

Unit 10 – Pattern and rhyme
Unit objective: Exploring pattern and rhyme in poetry

The Cow in the Storm

Name _____   Date _____

Cut out the pictures. Put them in the right order.

1	2	3
4	**5**	**6**

Unit 10 – Pattern and rhyme
Unit objective: Exploring pattern and rhyme in poetry

Name _____ Class _____ Date _____

		Type	AF	Mark
1	What does Tim do first? Tim washes his face. Tim fills the sink.	Literal	AF2	/1
2	Does Tim wash his face before he brushes his teeth? Yes No	Literal	AF2	/1
3	What does Tim do after he brushes his teeth? He turns off the tap. He washes his face.	Literal	AF3	/1
4	What do you do when you get ready for bed? Write three things you do before you get into bed. _____ _____ _____ _____ _____ _____	Visualisation	AF3	/6

Unit 1 – Familiar settings
Unit objective: Exploring events and characters in a setting

Total marks: /9

© Nelson Thornes 2009

Name _____ Class _____ Date _____

		Type	AF	Mark
1	Where does Adam sit to eat his sandwiches? Adam sits outside the café. Adam sits inside the café.	Literal	AF2	/1
2	Which animal does Adam feed? Adam feeds a sheep. Adam feeds a goat.	Literal	AF2	/1
3	What does Adam do at the playground? Adam plays on the slide. Adam plays on the swings.	Literal	AF2	/1
4	Two pictures need a sentence. Write a sentence saying what Adam is doing. _____ _____ _____ _____	Inference – deducing information	AF3	/4
5	Do you think Adam enjoyed his day out? Write a sentence saying 'why'. _____ _____ _____	Evaluation – empathy	AF6	/3

Name _____ Class _____ Date _____

		Type	AF	Mark
1	Ben is worried by the _____ . owl howl	Literal	AF2	/1
2	Pen thinks the howl is an _____ . cow owl	Literal	AF2	/1
3	Sue tells Ben to go to _____ . lie down sleep	Literal	AF2	/1
4	It is _____ howling. Spot Ben	Inference	AF3	/2
5	Copy a line that is repeated in the story. How many lines are repeated? _____ _____ _____ _____ _____	Analysis – text structure	AF4	/6

Unit 3 – Stories from home and far away
Unit objective: Recognising predictable, patterned language

Total marks: /11

© Nelson Thornes 2009

Instructions

Name _____ Class _____ Date _____

		Type	AF	Mark
1	The boy is making a _____ . drink banana split	Literal	AF2	/1
2	The boy pours squash into a _____ . mug glass	Literal	AF2	/1
3	The boy adds water from the _____ . tap jug	Literal	AF2	/1
4	The boy _____ the glass of squash. drinks gives away	Literal	AF2	/1
5	Write a list of what you need to make a glass of squash.	Inference	AF3	/4
6	Write some instructions for making a glass of squash.	Summarising	AF2 AF4	/4

Unit 5

Using the senses

Name _____ Class _____ Date _____

		Type	AF	Mark
1	What taste does the boy like? the taste of toothpaste the taste of sausages	Literal	AF2	/1
2	What sound does the girl like? the sound of bells the sound of the fairground	Literal	AF2	/1
3	What sight does the boy like? the sunshine flickering the fairground lights flashing	Literal	AF2	/1
4	Think of things you don't like to taste, smell, feel, hear and see. Choose and then describe one for each sense, starting each line with 'I don't like the ...' _____ _____ _____ _____ _____ _____ _____ _____ _____	Visualisation	AF3 AF5	/10

Total marks: /13

Name _____ Class _____ Date _____

		Type	AF	Mark
1	Where did Cinderella want to go? She wanted to go to the ball. She wanted to go outside.	Literal	AF2	/1
2	Who helped Cinderella? Her sisters helped. Her godmother helped.	Literal	AF2	/1
3	Who did Cinderella dance with? She danced with a friend. She danced with a prince.	Inference	AF3	/2
4	Did Cinderella leave the ball on time? No, she didn't leave on time. Yes, she left on time.	Inference	AF3	/2
5	Which story did you like best? Write a sentence saying why. _____ _____ _____ _____	Evaluation – opinion	AF6	/3

Name _____ Class _____ Date _____

			Type	AF	Mark
1	Barney likes to eat _____ . books shoes		Literal	AF2	/1
2	_____ forgot to put his shoes away. Dad Barney		Literal	AF2	/1
3	Barney chewed the shoes behind the _____. cupboard sofa		Literal	AF2	/1
4	Barney wasn't told off because he looked _____ . happy sorry		Literal	AF2	/1
5	Think of something that happened between you and an animal. Write about what happened.		Visualisation	AF3	/4

Unit 7 – Recounts
Unit objective: Understanding recounts and ordering events

Total marks: /8

© Nelson Thornes 2009

Name _____ Class _____ Date _____

		Type	AF	Mark
1	Who was Sophie having tea with? Sophie was having tea on her own.　　Sophie was having tea with her mummy.	Literal	AF2	/1
2	What noise did Sophie hear at the door? Sophie heard a ring.　　Sophie heard a knock.	Literal	AF2	/1
3	Who opened the door? Sophie opened the door.　　Mummy opened the door.	Literal	AF2	/1
4	What did the tiger want? The tiger wanted to meet Sophie.　　The tiger wanted to have tea.	Literal	AF2	/1
5	These words tell us about Sophie or the tiger. Choose the words to match Sophie. furry　big　pretty　stripy　hungry　polite	Visualisation	AF2	/2
6	These words tell us about Sophie or the tiger. Choose the words to match the tiger. furry　big　pretty　stripy　hungry　polite	Visualisation	AF2	/2

Name _____ Class _____ Date _____

		Type	AF	Mark
1	This _____ tells us what to do if we have an argument. story information	Analysis – text structure	AF4	/2
2	The first thing you should do is _____ arguing. stop keep	Literal	AF2	/1
3	_____ must have a turn to tell their story. Everyone One child	Literal	AF2	/1
4	Choose the best _____ to solve the argument. story idea	Literal	AF2	/1
5	Have you argued with a friend? What was it about? _____ _____ _____ _____ _____	Evaluation – previous experience	AF6	/3

Pattern and rhyme

Name _____ Class _____ Date _____

		Type	AF	Mark
1	What is the cow doing? The cow is sleeping.　　　The cow is chewing.	Literal	AF2	/1
2	What sound did the duck make? Quack　　　　　　　　Neigh	Literal	AF2	/1
3	What do the dogs do? The dogs dash.　　　　The dogs bark.	Literal	AF2	/1
4	When does the sun come out? At the start of the poem.　At the end of the poem.	Inference	AF3	/2
5	Which words rhyme with: 'black'? _____ 'barked'? _____ 'stopped'? _____	Analysis – language use	AF5	/3
6	Which cow poem do you like the best? _____ _____ _____ _____	Evaluation – opinion	AF6	/3

Using the Picture Snapshot Assessment

Donna Thomson

Reading and interpreting images provides a powerful and stimulating comprehension teaching and assessment tool for children of all ages and abilities. Pictures are full of inferred and hidden meaning and are a good starting point for comprehension instruction. This is because literal, inferential and evaluative visual clues are more immediate and easier to identify than text clues. Pictures can activate prior knowledge and experience in an instant. They prompt a range of emotions and personal reactions that absorb children and invite them to investigate and enquire further. The explicit teaching involved in the 'Snapshot Assessment' process helps children to develop essential thinking skills that can be transferred to other learning areas across the curriculum.

Picture Snapshot Assessment format

The 'Picture Snapshot Assessment' is an integral part of the **Nelson Comprehension** CD-ROMs. It provides an intriguing range of fiction and non-fiction stills and animated images with sound effects, accompanied by questions and answer guidance to test and assess a child's comprehension skills. The format is easy for pupils to use individually or in collaborative same- or mixed-ability groups of two to six pupils. It is also designed for teachers to use as a smart board instruction model. We have related the pictures to the APP assessment focuses 2 to 7 and have grouped them in levels which approximate to National Curriculum reading levels 1 to 5.

Assessing strengths and weaknesses

Childrens' responses to the questions, and their own enquiry about 'Snapshot' picture narratives, offer teachers an excellent opportunity to assess pupils' comprehension strengths and weaknesses. Assessment focus indicators that accompany each 'Snapshot' level provide teachers with a guide for assessment evidence gathered during each session. 'Snapshot' also assesses the comprehension skills of struggling decoders and pupils with language difficulties. The assessment process is effective because the absence of text (other than the title of a picture) allows the pupil the freedom to focus on comprehending, interpreting and choosing their own words to describe what is happening in a story, rather than on their struggle with decoding, which impedes their ability to understand the story in any depth.

Comprehension strategies

The 'Snapshot' activities are based on the Reciprocal Reading framework (Palicsar and Brown, 1986), a teacher-modelled scaffold that supports children's independent enquiry of fiction and non-fiction. Similarly, the 'Snapshots' are designed as an interactive process that helps children to read meaning within pictures, using the key comprehension strategies of summarising, predicting, questioning and clarifying. These key strategies draw on all assessment focuses except AF1. They encourage groups of the same or mixed ability pupils to delve deeply into picture narrative: extending their vocabulary, clarifying meaning and justifying viewpoints. It also helps them to develop the language of response and debate as they answer and generate their own literal, inferential and evaluative questions to monitor their understanding.

Using snapshots with small groups

While 'Snapshot' assessment is ideal for one-to-one assessment, it can also be used highly effectively with small groups of two to six pupils. If the children are unable to collaborate effectively, however, they will achieve little from the interactive activities. It can, therefore, be very useful to define a specific role for each child in the group (for example, a reader for the title and questions, a scribe, somebody to report back to the class, and someone to challenge their initial answers). Children can take it in turns to experience these roles as they move through the different levels.

How 'Snapshot' works

Each picture still and animated sequence is specifically selected to assess pupils' ability to use key comprehension strategies to answer questions and generate their own questions. The titles of the images relate to the picture and sound clues that are linked to the picture narrative. The purpose of this is to encourage the reader to link the word clues to the images and sounds to explain what is happening and to predict narrative outcomes.

Hotspots
The clues in the picture narrative that tell the reader 'what is happening', 'what may have happened before' or 'what may happen next' are referred to in the series as 'hotspots'. Teachers and children are able to confirm the meaning of each clue by clicking directly on the hotspot to reveal the information. These clues range from literal 'who?', 'what?, 'where?' information, to inferred

suggestions that require the reader to search for other clues to show how they have arrived at a conclusion, or why they think the characters are thinking or feeling in a certain way in the scene.

Screen 1 – section of whole image

The procedure on each level is progressive and extremely supportive. It begins with only part of the whole image shown on screen to encourage the reader to search for clues and link them to the title to predict what might be happening in the 'bigger picture' (rather like predicting contents from the cover of a book). The delving process also involves three literal questions that provide the basic information about the character(s), what they are doing and where they are; an evaluation question that asks them to consider what the characters might be feeling or thinking from their expression and body language; and a prediction question that asks them to calculate from the clues revealed what the story or 'whole scene' might be about.

Screen 1
Snapshot fiction level 2

Screen 2 – whole image

The next image reveals the whole picture and asks the reader to look carefully at new clues. The initial questions are revisited to allow the reader to revise their previous view of what is happening as they answer again. Finally, there are two prediction questions that help them to consider what might have happened before and after the 'whole picture' image.

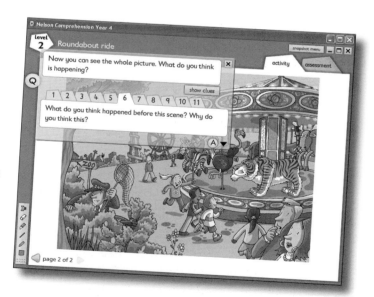

Assessment grid

The assessment at the end focuses on the accumulated answers to questions from screens 1 and 2, together with additional questions that ask the reader to generate their own query from a

Screen 2
Snapshot fiction level 2

given answer to further assess their understanding and to measure their ability to ask literal, inference and evaluation questions. The final assessment score indicates possible areas for teacher intervention.

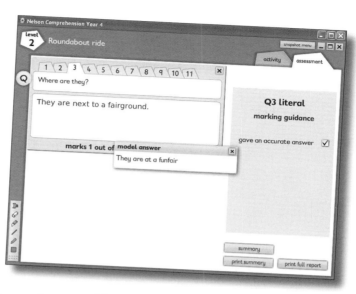

It is during the process of gathering and linking information to answer questions – and attempts at generating their own questions – that pupils' comprehension strengths and weaknesses are first exposed and the pupils themselves are able to identify areas of difficulty or lack of confidence. Throughout the process they are supported as they learn how to make links and connections between high and low levels of information.

Each assessment question is supported by a model answer and marking guidance.

'Snapshot' activities

The following levelled fiction and non-fiction 'snapshot' picture activities are designed to present a range of high- and low-level visual and sound clues that become more complex as the levels progress. Some are illustrations, others are black and white or colour photographs and many of them are animated. The purpose of these activities is to show children how to gather, clarify and organise information, how to identify the difference between literal and inferred meaning and how to make links and connections to solve problems. The animated clues have been included to draw the reader's eye to the hotspot information. The range of generic questions presented on each screen model a line of enquiry that the children soon learn and transfer to other areas of learning.

The first screen presents part of a whole picture. The reader first needs to read the title then look carefully at the picture for hotspot clues and listen for sound effects that suggest what may be happening in the narrative. The children's enquiry is guided by a series of questions that help them to gather information and make links of meaning between the clues on screens 1 and 2. The second screen shows the whole picture and includes further questions to support enquiry. These clues also provide confirmation of earlier predictions.

Snapshot: Level 1 Fiction – 'Halloween' (RA 5 yrs–6.5 yrs)

Visual type	Description
Colour illustration with some animation and sound effects	A pleasant looking woman is sitting in her cottage at the table pouring tea. It is night-time. Behind the woman we see children passing by, dressed in scary costumes. There are strange things happening in the room. There is loud banging at the door.

Screen information

Screen 1 – shows part of the whole picture

Screen 2 – the whole picture

What is happening?

The clues indicate that the children are 'trick-or-treating' because the title says it is Halloween. The children are dressed up in scary clothes and they are banging on the door and shouting 'trick-or-treat'. The clues also imply that the woman is a witch because of the hat and cloak on the door and strange goings-on in the house. The children are asked to consider what might happen if the witch opens the door to the children.

Hotspot clues: Black cat stirring pot, pouring green tea, children in ghost and skeleton outfits, lit pumpkin, moon in sky.

Sound clues: Bubbling cauldron, tea pouring, children's muffled laughter and chatter, loud banging on the door.

Hotspot clues: Children in skeleton and monster costumes, witch's hat and cloak, Halloween date on calendar – 31st October, walking butter dish, sweeping broom, jar of sweets and jar of spiders.

Sound clues: Loud banging on door, children's voices shouting 'trick or treat', 'swish' sound of brush on floor occasionally.

Snapshot: Level 1 Non-Fiction – 'Making Pizza' (RA 5 yrs–6.5 yrs)

Visual type	Description
Colour photograph with some sound effects	Four people working in a pizza factory.

Screen information

Screen 1 – shows part of the whole picture

Screen 2 – the whole picture

What is happening?

The clues indicate that the people are workers in a pizza factory because they are wearing protective clothing for hygiene reasons. They are all putting the same number of olives on pizzas in a line. There is the sound of machinery in the background and the title says 'Making Pizza'.

Hotspot clues: Girl in white coat, plastic hat, mouth covered, man holding olives in gloved hand, machinery, pizza.

Sound clues (screens 1 and 2): Background radio music, sound of machinery and movement of production line, occasional cough, muffled voice counting 1 … 2 … 3 … 4!

Hotspot clues: Pizza with four olives on, woman's hand reaching to put olives on bare pizza.

Snapshot: Level 2 Fiction – 'A Roundabout Ride' (RA 6.5 yrs–8.5 yrs)

Visual type
Colour illustration with some animations

Description
Outside a zoo by a funfair two zoo keepers are searching for something in the bushes. Children are running towards the roundabout ride. There is a tiger standing on the roundabout.

Screen information

Screen 1 – shows part of the whole picture

Screen 2 – the whole picture

What is happening?

The clues indicate that the two zoo keepers are looking for a tiger that has escaped from the zoo, because there are large paw prints leading to the roundabout where a tiger is standing. The tiger is pretending to be a ride on the roundabout either to avoid being caught by the zoo keepers, or because he is hungry and wants to trick a child into riding him so he can eat them – he is licking his lips. The reader is asked to consider what might happen next. Will the frightened onlookers tell the zoo keepers about the tiger before the children reach him?

Hotspot clues: Sign pointing to zoo, zoo keeper with net, zoo keeper moving branch to peer into shrub, large paw prints, helter skelter ride.

Sound clues (screens 1 and 2): Fairground music, children laughing and squealing, tiger licking lips, smacking sound, girl's excited voice saying 'I want to go on the tiger ride!'

Hotspot clues: Girl pointing at roundabout, end of tiger's tail twitching, tiger licking lips, girl on zebra ride looking worried, worried onlookers, excited children running up to roundabout.

Snapshot: Level 2 Non-Fiction – 'Dog Grooming' (RA 6.5 yrs–8.5 yrs)

Visual type
Colour Illustration with some sound effects

Description
The scene shows dogs being spruced up in a dog grooming parlour.

Screen information

Screen 1 – shows part of the whole picture

Screen 2 – the whole picture

What is happening?

The clues indicate that this is a place where dogs are washed and have their fur trimmed. The wagging tails tell us that most of them enjoy the experience, except the dog being showered. The clues further suggest that the dog owners take pride in the appearance of their dogs. The owner coming in looks embarrassed that his dog is so dirty compared to the perfect poodle going out.

Hotspot clues: Perfect-looking poodle, dirty and scruffy-looking dog, 'Posh Paws' writing backwards on glass door, dog owner coming in – expression on his face (comparing the two dogs), dog owner going out – expression on her face (comparing the two dogs).

Sound clues (screens 1 and 2): Buzz of electric trimmer, sound of shower spray, voice saying 'Good dog', dog barking, dog whining.

Hotspot clues: Two dogs ready to go home, electric trimmer, clipped fur (falling chunks of hair), girl's uniform ('Posh Paws' logo), man holding shower head, all dogs (except one in bath) have wagging tails.

Snapshot: Level 3 Fiction – 'All at Sea' (RA 8.5 yrs–10.5 yrs)

Visual type
Animated colour illustration with sound effects

Description
A boat has overturned in a choppy sea. A man who was hanging on in the water is now sitting on top of the boat calling for help. There is a man in a small boat nearby who is pulling another man out of the water. A person is watching from the shore.

Screen information

Screen 1 – shows part of the whole picture

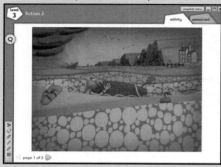

Screen 2 – the whole picture

What is happening?
The clues indicate that two men are out for the day and were just about to have lunch when their boat was overturned during a bad storm. Further clues suggest that a man in a small boat has come from the shore to rescue them, because someone is watching from the shore as he pulls one of the men into the boat. Another clue implies that the man who is calling for help may not be a strong swimmer, because unlike the other man, he has chosen not to swim to safety. The reader is asked to consider what might happen to him in the end.

Hotspot clues: Overturned boat, hand clutching boat rope, top of head (turning to look at other boat), wave swell, floating apple, lunchbox, floating oar, life jacket, lightning/dark clouds, seagulls.

Sound clues: Seagulls crying, voice in panic to himself 'Oh no, it's getting closer', sound of wind/waves/sea.

Hotspot clues: Frightened man jumps up onto boat, shark's fin circling boat, man pulling swimmer into boat, man swimming towards boat, person watching on shore.

Sound clues: Voice shouts out 'Help – over here!', sound of wind/waves/sea, seagulls crying, oar banging against boat.

Snapshot: Level 3 Non-Fiction – 'Fish for Dinner' (RA 8.5 yrs–10.5 yrs)

Visual type
Black and white photograph with sound effects

Description
Two men are in a moored boat and a dog is watching them from a jetty.

Screen information

Screen 1 – shows part of the whole picture

Screen 2 – the whole picture

What is happening?
The sound clues indicate that the two men in the moored boat are French and out fishing for the day. The photograph is black and white, which suggests it is a scene from the past, and the men are smoking pipes and using old-fashioned equipment to fish with. The title implies that the men are not the only ones expecting fish for dinner – the dog is whining and looks like he is waiting for something as he watches them fishing.

Hotspot clues: Boat tied to mooring post, heaped rocks, fishing rod, hatch cover, dog with collar looking at something going on.

Sound clues (screens 1 and 2): 'Swish' sound of line being cast, 'plop!' sound as hook and bait hit the water, men talking in French, sighing and chuckling, whining sound.

Hotspot clues: Man sitting on left of boat, man sitting on chair smoking pipe, old-fashioned bamboo fishing rod, old-fashioned containers, man wearing French beret.

Analysing responses to questions

Gathering information, discussing and retelling is an essential part of the comprehension process. It is the first indicator of a reader's real engagement and basic understanding of the text or picture narrative. It shows how observant they are and what sort of reasoning skills they have. If they haven't grasped the main ideas when summarising the story information, the indications are that they are not looking closely enough; have poor language skills (vocabulary/phrasing) and sequencing ability; or have little personal or prior experience that links to the information in the picture. They may, as a consequence, give limited answers to the following questions about the picture narrative. The teacher may choose to give the individual or group a less demanding (lower level) picture to work from.

Level 3 Fiction snapshot 'All at Sea'

In the process of determining whether a student has answered a question correctly, the teacher needs to consider the following points.

- Does the reader's answer relate to the information in the title and picture?
- Is prior knowledge or experience being used to help explain a picture narrative?
- Does the reader understand the vocabulary used in the question?
- Does the reader have problems gathering literal or inferred information in response to questions?
- Does the reader have problems making links between clues to arrive at a conclusion?
- Is the reader engaged in the picture narrative?

Analysing responses to question types

Example: Level 4 'Good Fit' (Screen 2 picture)

Literal – explicit meaning – Who?, What?, Where? Right there! Information that is obvious and does not require interpretation.

Literal questions ask for answers that are found directly on the page. This simple form of questioning is essential when assessing whether a reader understands how to link key enquiry words in a question to basic key information within the text.

An example of a poor response to a literal question:

Question: *What* are the characters *doing* with the large roll of *material*?

Answer: The characters are making clothes.

Comment

The answer given here is an inferred response rather than an answer to a literal question. An inference question would need to include 'How do you know that?' to elicit this answer and evidence from the reader to support it.

The detail is clear in the picture. Although the reader has understood that many of the characters are *doing* something with material, they have not read the question carefully enough to identify who the question is directed at. The enquiry refers to the 'characters with the large roll of material' in the foreground of the picture and asks *what they are doing*.

Correct answer: The *characters* are **carrying** the *large roll of material*.

Inference/Prediction – implied/hidden meaning. Information that is suggested within the narrative. The reader is required to think and search for clues that offer evidence to back up their response to questions.

Inference is not a straightforward question type. Although it allows for a variety of answers, all responses require evidence that relates to the picture or text information (in the title) and illustrator's/photographer's intention to support their answers. Answers that do not refer directly to the picture narrative are not acceptable – however reasonable and plausible.

An example of two poor responses to an inference question:

Question: Are the *people* in the picture *making clothes* for a *giant*? How do you know that?

Answer 1: Yes.

Answer 2: Yes, because they have drawn a picture of him.

Comment

The first response does not fully answer the question because the second part of the question asks them to give evidence that shows how they know the answer is 'yes'.

The second response is incorrect because the reader has not considered the question closely enough. They have not accurately identified the clues in the question – *people, making clothes, giant* – and linked them to the inferred clues in the picture narrative – *little people, measuring and sewing material, clothes pattern, giant feet* – to provide an answer that is supported by clear evidence. In addition, it is helpful for readers to know that if they use part of the question to answer with, it will guide their answers and help to keep them on the right track.

> Correct answer: *Yes, the **people** in the picture are **making clothes for a giant**. I know this because there is a pair of **giant feet** in the picture and next to them much **smaller** people are **cutting** and **sewing large rolls of material** from a **clothes pattern** designed for a **very large man**.*

Evaluation – personal meaning. What you think characters may be feeling, doing or thinking from clues within the narrative and your own experience of life. Expressing an opinion based on information given.

Evaluation questions vary considerably according to the reader's own experience and prior knowledge. However, whatever their response, it must relate to the information given in the picture to be acceptable.

An example of two poor responses to an evaluation question:

> Question: *Do you think* some of the *characters* are *finding their task difficult*? *Why* do you say that?
>
> Answer 1: Yes.
>
> Answer 2: No, because I think the design they are using looks easy to understand.

Comment

The first answer is incomplete because the person has not given a reason for their answer. The second response is inappropriate. The reader has not focused on all the key words in the question. Instead they have based their answer too much on personal opinion that is not supported by evidence from the picture. Although the reader has considered whether the '*task*' is '*difficult*', they have not linked this to the other key clue in the question that refers to the '*characters*' in the picture. Consequently, they have not looked for facial expressions and body language in the picture that suggest how the characters might be feeling or thinking about *'their task'*.

Appropriate answer: *Yes, I think some of the characters are finding their task difficult because* **they are puzzling** *over the clothes design and* **looking unsure** *about it.*

Clarification – understanding the meaning of vocabulary or a concept within the context of picture narrative. Defining the meaning of a word or concept from evidence available in a picture.

Readers of 'Snapshot' are asked to infer and define the meaning for words or ideas in the images by making links with clues in the picture narrative.

Level 4 'Good fit'
Screen 2

An example of a poor response to a clarification question:

Question: There is a small man in the picture using a *megaphone*. Explain *what* he is using this *device* for.

Answer: He is using a megaphone because he is making a long distance phone call.

Comment

The reader has answered the question incorrectly because although he has used prior knowledge to try to guess the meaning of the word, he has not referred to clues in the picture that suggest *what the device is* and *what it is being used for.* His answer does not make sense in the context of the picture.

Correct answer: *The small man in the picture is using a megaphone to make his* **tiny voice** *louder so the tailors who are measuring the giant* **high above** *him* **can hear what he is saying**.

Assessing levels – marking

Each comprehension level is a based on marks out of 20 that are represented as a percentage score at the end of the assessment, for example 2/20 = 10%; 12/20 = 60% and so on. The marks range from 1–3 points according to the question type. The marks for question types can be correlated with the QCA SATs marking system and are as follows:

- Literal: 1 point
- Inference: 2 points
- Prediction: 2 points
- Clarification: 2 points
- Evaluation: 3 points

The reader's total score represents a snapshot of their ability to gather information, summarise, predict, clarify and finally ask and answer literal, inferential and evaluative questions from pictures and titles. Ability within each level is measured to establish whether the reader or group need to drop down a level to help them to develop their comprehension skills further; need to remain at the same level to receive further instructional support; or are accomplished enough to move on to challenges on the next level. This can be used as evidence for a periodic assessment of the children's comprehension skills.

Comprehension ability within level

Easy/secure	score 70–100%	(move to next level)
Instructional/partial	score 40–65%	(remain at this level)
Hard/insecure	score 0–35%	(move down a level)

Notes

Notes

Notes